HONOR IN THE

GOSPEL:

A Theological Discussion on a Critical Issue

ASHEY WANDERA

HONOR IN THE GOSPEL:

A Theological Discussion on a Critical Issue

Cover Design: Bedford Buyungo; buyungobedford@gmail.com

Editor: Rebecca Rugyendo; agiriug@gmail.com

ISBN: 978-9970-9899-0-4

First Printed in Uganda

To Oliver Nantumbwe Tolofiisa, my mother. Although now in eternity, you were the perfect pattern of honor that I watched from the day I was born to the day you entered glory. I will forever honor you.

CONTENTS

ACKNOWLEDGEMENTS

Since this book is about honor, in no chronological order, I would like to honor the following people that have helped me during the writing of this book, and those that have walked with me at a certain point along the path of my life.

USA

Pastor Cates Noles and your wife Beverly of Rainsville Alabama and Mr. Kenny Dicxon; thank you for hosting me and giving me a conducive environment from which I could write this book. You are people of integrity.

Pastor Clay and Andrea Bishop in Manchester Kentucky, thank you for hosting and allowing me to think and write this book. Clay, I celebrate your friendship, brotherhood and wisdom. Pastor Donald Sims through whom I met Clay and Papa Apostle Rick Clendenen, I cannot forget your faith in me.

Apostle Charlie and Senior Pastor Vikki Ammons of RCC in Newport News Virginia, you welcomed me in your house, hosted me in the "Bishop's Chambers", giving me the time and space I needed to write most of this content. Thank you!

Precious Namazzi, thank you for hosting me in California and for driving me to Bethel Church in Redding. Visiting Bethel in November 2017 was an unforgettable experience.

Pastor Jeff and Sherri Hundley in Lenoir City, TN, thank you for honoring my invitation as the very first missions' team I hosted in Uganda (and especially accepting to come to Gulu in May 2017). Thank you for believing in me.

Momma Sue Hubbard Smith of Mission Minded Ministries in Kentucky, the prophecy you gave me in 2006 still rings a bell in my spirit.

My mentors in Manitoba Canada; Apostle Ray Deurkeson and

Pastor Stefan Deurkeson, Church Renewal is a work of God. I am honored to be part of it.

UGANDA

Different men and women of God have impacted my life at different seasons.

My spiritual father, Bishop Solomon Mukonjo of Church of God Kamwokya in Kampala, you taught me how to honor all men through your life. Your input and advise in this book was implemented.

Apostle Alex Mitala of BBT Mission in Nansana-Wakiso; the things you have done for and taught me, and the things you do for the kingdom of God, these pages are not enough to fill them up.

Apostle John Bunjo of Christian Restoration Ministries, I keep to memory the years I served under your ministry and sat under your mentorship. Those were very hard years in my life, but you encouraged me to persevere. James Kisakye, it was through Apostle Bunjo's ministry that I met you. Thank you for becoming a brother I was not born with.

Pastor Michael Kyazze of Omega Healing Center in Kampala, I honor you for impacting my life in my early years. You are a great example of devotion, discipline, and consistence.

Apostle Kato "Katc" Yusuf in Copenhagen Denmark, coming in the life of my friends and I was God-ordained. Ivan and Stephen, thank you for your input and advise after writing my first draft.

Apostle Grace Lubega of Phaneroo Ministries International; your sermons, devotions, wisdom and the two times I have met you in person have greatly impacted my life.

Prophet Elvis Mbonye of Zoe Fellowship Ministries, God used you to set me on the right path towards my destiny through the accurate word of knowledge and prophecy you gave me in 2016.

My family; Joan, Andrew, Ivan and Leah, I honor you.

Agnes Namaganda, I appreciate your advice and input. Robert Bake, I cannot forget the few minutes I sat in your office and you perused through this book. They were the inspiration behind the introduction of this book.

My awesome editor, Rebecca Rugyendo, may the Lord make your name great upon the face of the earth and give you all your heart's desires. My graphics designer, Brian Bedford Buyungo, what would I do without you? Your work is award-winning.

Thank you Pastor Moses "Mosze" Mukisa, the senior leader of Worship Harvest Ministries which started Harvest Institute, for your visionary and exceptional leadership. Thank you Harvest Institute for "stretching me" beyond measure. This has enabled me to exercise my potential and ability. My Assessor, Blessed Ivan Muhumuza, thank you for the patience, advice, longsuffering and encouragement you gave me. I knew I would write a book someday, but Harvest Institute made 2018 the "future" in which I wrote and released my first book.

Pastor Richard Magongo of Exceller's Chapel Kampala, and my former lecturer at university during my first year; thank you for recognizing my writing ability.

Henry Wynn Kakooza, thank you for being one of my small innermost circle of friends. You recognized my ability to write and helped me actualize it through this book. Your input and advise in this book is appreciated. You are a true brother and bestman indeed!

Martha Birungi Wandera; my wife, my life partner, my attorney, my best friend, my advisor and mother to our awesome children (Genessa and Jezreel), thank you! I am so grateful that you believed in me enough to marry me. Thank you for allowing me to fulfill the call of God upon my life. You have made my life so beautiful. You are a virtuous woman, I honor you.

ENDORSEMENTS

Ashey Wandera has given us a cultural and biblical discussion on the subject of Honor. Having traveled through many countries in Europe and Africa, I have seen the many forms and customs that he describes in the book. Honor is an objective view of the practices that some may see as excessive or inappropriate. Even in the United States, ceremonies that include biblical practices such as foot washing are not always understood or appreciated by believers. *Honor in the Gospel* outlines the scriptures and instances that would demonstrate a clear purpose for honor in spiritual relationships. The book methodically measures the acts against biblical teachings and kingdom culture to assess their validity. This book is a great resource to anyone wanting to understand the power and purpose of giving and receiving honor. It will guide you in honoring those who have achieved, and encouraging others who are moving toward a higher calling.

Chaplain Randy Jarmon,
World Outreach Center Church of God,
Newport News, Virginia, USA

Most people live in an atmosphere void of honor and desperately seek help in creating such a culture. The need is real and the desire is genuine. The church has for the longest time been in need of reconstruction. Our notions of "Kingdom government" need to be conceptually and structurally redefined. Our heart language for kingdom definition needs to be revisited and restated and it is out of our hearts that we will speak and live. Ashey Wandera in his book, *Honor in the Gospel* gives us an inspired, informed and biblical approach to understanding what needs to be the heart culture of the kingdom. An essential read for those who desire supernatural fruitfulness and I believe that fruitfulness will come out of the context of honor.

Gerald Rovis Masinde,
Lead Pastor, Bethel Covenant Connection Ministries,
Kampala, Uganda

Honor in the Gospel is a great book giving an in-depth analysis on issues of honor, hence giving an answer to the many questions in the minds of the children of God across the world. One of these questions is on "spiritual fathers", something that Ashey answers extensively well. I highly recommend this book to every child of God, especially those in leadership so that they can raise up effective and powerful priests and kings for the kingdom of God who are honor-conscious in this generation.

Fred Mwesigye,
Senior Pastor,
House of God Church Entebbe, Uganda

After reading my brother Ashey Wandera's Facebook post, my spirit sensed a budding gifted writer of our generation. Wandera's balanced analysis on the subject of honor in his book *Honor in the Gospel* provides a wonderful resource for teachers, pastors and Christians to differentiate between honor and idolatry. The different cultural perspectives and building a culture of honor are key subjects every pastor should teach; your church will learn how to honor you and give honor to each other. What more can a pastor ask for? *Honor in the Gospel* is a must read. God bless you as you enjoy this wonderful work.

Richard Magongo;
Lead Pastor,
Excellers Chapel Kampala, Uganda

A pleasurable read full of credible and well-researched information for those of us who want to fully investigate the meaning of honor in the gospel; who to honor, and how to honor them, considering how it was practiced then and how it is presented today. Ashey Wandera takes readers to the heights of biblical, cultural and traditional perspectives of honor and its possible impacts. This is a must-read book on honor in this contemporary world. Read this book and learn from the author.

Alex Mwesigwa Mitala Epaphroditus
Missions Director,
Back to the Bible Truth Evangelistic Mission Uganda

Ashey Wandera has provided for us a new and much needed lens through which to view the subject of honor in the gospel. While covering this controversial yet critical topic, this book presents a theologically-alert, biblically-grounded, comprehensive study that deserves the attention of the church in our time. It seems the church at large has been more affected by our various cultural influences and presuppositions than we have scripture when it comes to the issue of honor. While Ashey takes into account cultural perspectives on the topic, he ultimately steers us through any confusion so that we arrive at a healthy biblical understanding of a kingdom culture of honor. From pastors and leaders to new converts, this book will open your eyes to the heart of God and all that He has to say about true honor. I highly recommend this book as I believe it will sow seeds of restoration for this Christian virtue that is on the verge of being lost.

Clay Bishop,
Associate Pastor,
City of Hope Church Manchester, KY, USA.

I believe that honor is the key to the treasury of heaven. Through honor, we release God's favor, His finances, and His future into our lives. Ashey Wandera is just such a man. I have witnessed his servant heart as he worked behind the scenes to faithfully honor those in leadership above him and to prove himself a worthy steward by faithfully caring for those things that belonged to another. Now, God has given him his own. This great book you hold in your hand is a compilation of the lessons he has learned and the wisdom by which he applied them. He has been able to strike a keen balance between true Biblical honor and hero worship of men. I believe that as you read and apply these Biblical principles in your own life; you, too, will become a vessel of honor in the house of the Lord and meet for the Master's use.

Apostle Rick Clendenen,
Author and Church Planter;
Kentucky, USA.

In 2015 I was moved by God to plant a church in Kira town, Wakiso district, in Uganda. Ashey was among the seven people on my launch team. I knew he was a leader with a higher lid than mine, but he honored and served me because I was the team leader. He gave 100 percent while serving with me, while in charge of our school of ministry where he raised up leaders who are serving today. In 2018 we prayed for him to go start a ministry in Gulu and I blessed him. So, there is no better person to talk about honor than this man.

Stephen Mukonjo
Team Leader;
Ignite Life Ministries Kira; Wakiso, Uganda
Tutor; Ignite Life Bible School Fort-portal, Uganda.

Honor in the Gospel confronts us with the context of honor in the Body of Christ. Its place has not been lost so much as it has been ignored. Highlighting unforgettable biblical encounters that prompted glorious impartations, the writer helps us to identify a serious deficit that obstructs some power episodes in many Christian settings today. With its gentle rebuke and correction, the book encourages and challenges the discerning believer to give honor to whom honor is due, in the place and time in which it is due.

Gloria Amagu Kisekka,
Senior Leader; Field of Harvest Ministries,
Arua, Uganda

Many people have written about honor, but Ashey Wandera has not only pulled out fresh insights out of a well-known concept, but also challenges us in many ways over a subject that the Church has mixed reactions about. This practical and challenging book will compel us to give honour where it is due. Thank you Ashey!

Ivan Kisakye Wandera,
Field Director; Vast Grace Missions Uganda.
Tutor; Ignite Life Bible School Fort-portal, Uganda.

Honor in the Gospel is very well written. Honor is something I have not thought too much about except to try to withdraw from it. I have never wanted honor or recognition from men. My philosophy has been, "let all the honor and glory go to Christ, who deserves it all." I have for the most part thought that honor and respect go hand in hand. Ashey Wandera has brought out a new concept for us.

If we could all put honor in action and work as teams instead of separate entities, we would accomplish much for the kingdom of God. I am afraid we fall short and look for people like ourselves and our church rather than the simple believers from all churches. In my heart and my spirit, I feel that this is a good book for young ministers or even lay workers. I highly recommend it.

Sue Hubbard Smith,
President; Mission Minded Ministries,
Kentucky, USA.

-- - - - - - -   -- - - - - - -   -- - - - - -   -- - - - - - -

Insightful and thought provoking. Brother Ashey Wandera releases information and revelation that brings to light some key principles that allow us to be more kingdom-minded and more kingdom-focused. When leaders operate in honor, then honor should be reciprocated. Proper honor with understanding releases harmony and cooperation in relationships and leadership in the Body of Christ.

You will love how that as each chapter unfolds you are taken on a journey to better understand the position and condition that leaders should and must take in order to be in proper fellowship and communion with those who are directly and indirectly connected to them. Honor is not for those who demand it! It is given to those who deserve it.

First of all, I highly recommend this book because I know first-hand the character of its writer.

Secondly, it is a powerful book with excellent revelation that is sure to stir your mind and spirit as it unveils powerful truths and challenges as well as great and valuable information. The Holy Spirit's DNA is definitely all over the pages of this book. You will be a better leader and a better person as you enjoy this must read!

Jerry Lewis,
Senior Pastor; Freedom Christian Fellowship Church,
London KY, USA.

- - - -- - - - - - - - -- - - - - - - -- - - - - - - -- - - - - -

From the very moment I met Ashey Wandera, I immediately noticed his hunger for knowledge, and his love for Christ. He asked questions that demanded more than a generic answer and participated in discussions that required me to engage. In this book, I think you will find all these qualities and characteristics in the way he writes.

Pastor Cates Noles,
Senior Pastor; Rainsville Community Church,
Rainsville, Alabama, USA.

- - - - - - -- - - - - - - -- - - - - - - -- - - - - -

I highly esteem and salute my brother, Ashey Wandera, for spending countless hours, unveiling a very necessary subject of our time. As you read this book, you are not only acquiring knowledge, but you will encounter the truth perhaps, that you had never paid attention to. I have read it and found out that it is priceless.

Honor in The Gospel will help you understand the privileges, blessings and anointing that come with rewarding someone for their difference from you. The concept of honor here vividly and in a unique way expresses the basic Christian attitude towards God, parents, leaders and society. You will learn that when something costs you something, you will honor it.

I perceive honor as the very act of esteeming or showing respect to someone greater than ourselves. God says, "A son honors his father and a servant his master. If then I am the Father, where is My honor?" (Malachi 1:6). You might say some people are not honorable, but we honor not because people have done what is pleasing and good to us; instead, we honor because of the authority they carry.

After reading this book, you will not see your spiritual father the same way you did and if you have not recognized one, this book will teach you how to discern them and render to them the honor due to them.

Therefore, without hesitation, I endorse and honor my brother and friend, whom I have known for almost 3 decades for presenting this awesome book to us. Read it with an open heart. The Author is giving us more than the information; it's his lifestyle.

Henry Wynn Kakooza,
President; Vast Grace Missions
Gayaza, Wakiso, Uganda

- - - - - -- - - - - - -- - - - - - -- - - - - - -- - -

I have thoroughly enjoyed reading *Honor in the Gospel* by Ashey Wandera. It is rare in Christendom today to come upon a theological discussion on such a topic as 'honor'. From culture to Christ, Ashey works to give a complete view of the subject and gives credence of both for and against. His style of writing gives you the ability to use this resource as a tool for discussion, studying, and preparation in understanding multiple aspects of the issue. I believe that you will love this book, not only in its first light, but also in the many times you refer back to its foundational elements.

I highly encourage any leader to read this book and offer it as a reflective resource to those who are serving in ministry with them. My personal knowledge of this young apostle gives me hope for all nations and people that come in contact with him. He truly has a heart for the Kingdom of God, Uganda, and the world. I am honored to be a part of his life and ministry. (See there, I have used aspects of his book even in this endorsement. Already a student).

Apostle Wayne Lee Junior,
Senior Leader; Worship Life Jasper,
President; Worship Life International,
Alabama, USA

- - - - - - - - - - - - - - - - - - - -- - - - - - -- - - - - -

It is with the highest honor that I endorse this amazing masterpiece entitled, *"Honor In The Gospel."* I believe this book is a must read for all believers regardless of denominational affiliation, cultural background or racial profile. Honor is a gift and a mandate from God! It is often spoken of from pulpits across the nations, but I am not sure if it is understood or put into practice the way God truly intended. Apostle Ashey Wandera has stepped into the portals of heaven and come out with a clear view on what honor is and how it should be exercised and restored as a biblical mandate and principle in the body of Christ!

The content is vast and not produced by a novice, but by one who practices what he preaches. Apostle Ashey is a man of high honor, dignity and integrity. He is qualified to write this book because it is truly a snapshot of his life. Don't wait! Don't procrastinate! Go out and get this book and begin teaching it in your bible classes and leadership trainings. I believe in honor and I believe in this book!

Apostle Charlie Ammons;
Apostolic Leader; Restoration Christian Church,
Newport News,
Virginia,
USA

FOREWORD

In 1989, I met a humble, diligent and deeply rooted Christian lady who lived just a few meters from our church. She brought to me her two sons Ivan and Ashey and asked me to be their pastor; a duty which I took on with much delight because this is the calling on my life.

I didn't just pastor them — I took them on as my own and saw them grow up. Ashey was just five years at the time and even at such a tender age, he always amazed me with his level of thinking, understanding and creativity.

As a teenager, he was one of my best disciples; who never relented and even in the face of many challenges, and with all humility he always worked hard to get things done. He was an apostle in the making. He was relational, situational and intentional in his motives. I saw a great leader in him.

With that background, his book, *"Honor in the Gospel"* is filled with knowledge and understanding because he has spent all his life in the gospel and on his journey, he has had several mentors whom he honors.

Today, the understanding people have about honoring God is not so minimal, the tricky bit is about how to honor the "men of God," who have sometimes been honored beyond the acceptable limits. This has made them seem like demi-gods; an act that reveals a total mix-up in the whole practice. I will attribute this to their immaturity in the understanding of the Word in its entirety and a lack of scriptural guidance among most people in the congregations.

The word of God is a yardstick and measuring rod that we use so that we don't error as we practice honor. The great commission requires us to make disciples (molding to spiritual maturity) and not just converts, which is not the case in most churches today. The immature believers have a poor discernment faculty and most at times will fall prey to false leadership and doctrines that will impart the wrong practice of honor into them.

Those who seek to receive honor from people are self-serving-leaders while those who refuse extreme honor given to them by the people are servant-leaders. God called servant-leaders, that is why He says that when you deny yourself, you become His disciple and leader indeed (Refer to Matthew 20:25-28). The attitude and response of Paul and Barnabas when people wanted to venerate them as gods is commendable. We need to learn from them.

This book by my true son in the Lord addresses issues such as these and more, and I guarantee you that if you read and digest all that is written on these pages, you will know the true, biblical and rightful honor.

Bishop Solomon Mukonjo,
Senior Pastor;
Church of God Kamwokya,
Kampala, Uganda

INTRODUCTION

The thought of writing this book started from a Facebook Note I wrote in September 2017 after I had responded to a hot debate among the Christian community in my country (Uganda) that had been raging on social media concerning honor. Accusations and counter-accusations had been thrown about concerning the way Christians perceived the art of honoring men of God. While one camp did not find a problem with the methods and activities that surround the culture of honor in the church; especially the way Christians honor their spiritual leaders, others were enraged at them! In the years that have gone by, a battle has ensued on whether the church (as disciples of Jesus Christ) is following the example of her Master (Jesus), who honored people by serving them and washing his disciples' feet or just playing around.

One early morning, on September 7, 2017, the Spirit of God woke me up and instructed me to write a note on what the scriptures speak about honor. The long Facebook note had scriptural references to the acts of honor I found in the Bible, offering my thoughts on each of them. Two of my friends who read that note told me that I had argued very well, and that I could be a good writer! The writing did not happen until I had enrolled at an institute of leadership where I undertook to write about this subject as part of a class assignment. I chose to develop that Facebook note into the book you are holding in your hands right now.

Honor is a very diverse subject in and outside the Bible. The southern states in the USA used to practice what has been branded as "Honor-Shame Culture"; which involved personal dignity, protecting of family names, control, shame, threats, shunning, "honor-balance", and revenge dynamics.

Research has been done on this subject by a number of psychologists from around the world, and some cultures (e.g in Japan) still practice

Honor-Shame, coupled with its "honor suicides". This book, however, is not about this kind of "Honor". It focuses on the biblical act of giving and receiving esteem, value and regard in human relationships. Biblical honor is not a one-way privilege to be given to only those in leadership positions and "five-fold offices."

In my country Uganda, whenever we have had different scandals in the Body of Christ, apart from a few TV and radio appearances, and a few print and social media articles and posts here and there, no one ever comes out to give a biblical, scholarly, well researched, and exegetical response to any issue that the Body might be facing at the time. This book is one of the very few books written in Uganda on a critical issue that has conflicting debates around it. It handles honor from different angles.

Biblical honor is something that I think hasn't been well addressed. There is ignorance, controversies, and lack of knowledge surrounding it. This book shows the way culture and traditions influence how we honor one another by asking; "what is the relationship between being a Christian and one's culture and traditional orientation?"

It also answers the following questions:
- What is the Biblical perspective on honor?
- How can we build and cultivate a kingdom culture of honor?
- How do we honor one another as kings and priests?
- What is the role of the body of Christ in relation to society?
- Why is humility the true mark of spiritual leadership? Because if, as a leader in the local body, people honor me, and I consider myself to be irreplaceable, infallible, and indispensable, then I have got it wrong. It is not humility leading but pride, yet God resists the proud but gives grace to the humble.

Furthermore, the book explains that as we honor each other, the person that is receiving the honor doesn't have to use it as leeway because honor is not a privilege; but a blessing and a gift. Spiritual relationships are very crucial in the body of Christ. This book discusses "spiritual fathers" and "spiritual sons", so that we build and cultivate healthier spiritual relationships. What is the responsibility of spiritual fathers to their spiritual sons and vise versa? The book digs deep into this highly debatable teaching on "spiritual fathers".

Two more critical issues in honor that normally go unnoticed are discernment and impartation. How many people understand what true discernment really is? Yet one must correctly discern the people they are going to submit to and honor because of a spiritual transaction that happens between the one that honors, and the one that is honored. This is called impartation.

In winding up the book, I also talk about the biblical representations, manifestations and expressions of honor. Answering questions like; how is honor represented, manifested, and expressed in the bible? What are the practices and blessings of honor? How about those who elevate and venerate ministers of God into demi-gods by giving them all sorts of titles and names? Should they keep doing it just because they have "freedom in Christ" and understand "spiritual mysteries"? Shouldn't there be caution and some level of discipline so as to avoid offending the weaker brethren?

Is celebration the same as idol worship? What are honor's extremes? How much honor is extreme? Who determines what is extreme? If honor is scriptural, who should set the rules, guidelines and regulations for it? Should the State interfere with freedom of worship because of it? Who determines how people should honor their spiritual leaders? What is the whole council of God on honor? Is it possible to honor God without honoring one another?"

If scriptures say touch not my anointed, isn't there a place for correction? Can't we correct one another in the body of Christ? But what is true Biblical correction? How do we correct one another? Christ sets the precedence, and so does Paul. This book will show how true correction is done.

A shocking scripture is given in Jude 8-11 talking about blasphemous people who speak evil and dishonor dignitaries. In that portion of scripture, Jude, inspired by the Spirit of God, mentions Satan as an example of a dignitary! He says that when both Satan and the Arch-Angel Michael were disputing over the body of Moses, Michael did not bring a slanderous accusation against Satan, but only said, "The LORD rebuke thee Satan." This got me wondering; should celestial beings be honored?

Such issues and more are what this book is all about.

Enjoy your reading.

Ashey Wandera,
Kampala, Uganda
March 2019

CHAPTER 1

BIBLICAL AND CULTURAL PERSPECTIVES OF HONOR

"It is sanctified by coming from His holy hand; it is dignified by following his most wise and just disposal; it is fortified and assured by depending on His unquestionable Word, and uncontrollable power: who, as He is the prime author of all good, so He is in a special manner the sovereign dispenser of honor." [1]

"It is important, therefore, not to assume that a single definition of honor can apply to every biblical text." [2]

Defining Honor from a Biblical, Hebrew Perspective

This book is a theological discussion that presents honor as the Bible teaches it. Honor, as taught in the Bible, is a very wide word that has a number of meanings and applications. We shall first briefly look at its Biblical Hebrew root meaning, perspective, and application.

A highly reputable Biblical Scholar, W.E Vine, in his Complete Expository Dictionary of Old and New Testament Words, writes:

---

[1] The Theological Works of Isaac Barrows, Volume I, Sermon VI: The Reward of Honoring God, Page 249

[2] Moxnes, H; Honor and Shame: An Essay, University of Oslo, Page 12

1

"The Biblical Word "Honor", comes from a Hebrew root word, "kabod" [as a noun] which means, "honor; glory; great quantity; multitude; wealth; reputation [majesty]; splendor." "Kabod" appears about 200 times in Biblical Hebrew. A related word, "kabed", [as a verb], also means "to be heavy, weighty, honored, glorious" and appears about 150 times in the Hebrew Bible. This idea [of "kabed"] also explains how the word can be used to indicate the state of "being honored" or "glorious," for honor and glory are additional qualities that are added to a person or thing. "To honor" or "glorify" anything is to add something which it does not have in itself, or that which others can give (Some additional explanatory brackets are mine).

From this description by Vine, it is evident that "honor" is a result of the value added to something or someone, which value was not inherent in the thing itself or individual themselves. The same root word is attributed to the honor due to God, though this kind of honor in the context of the scripture where the word occurs is absolute, ultimate and distinct because it involves and is defined by worship and adoration, which should not be attributed to man or a thing. If the honor due to God is attributed to a man or an object, then it becomes idolatry.

God as the Source of Honor

"
If the honor due to God is attributed to a man or an object, then it becomes idolatry...
"

1 Chronicles 29:12: *"Wealth and honor come from you; you are the ruler of all things. In your hands are strength and power to exalt and give strength to all (NIV)."*

Biblical honor is from the LORD. Before anyone ever receives honor of any kind from another, the

LORD has to first give it to them.

Many people have given themselves names in many spheres of life, but have still not been honored. Others work extremely hard to earn honor, but do not get it still.

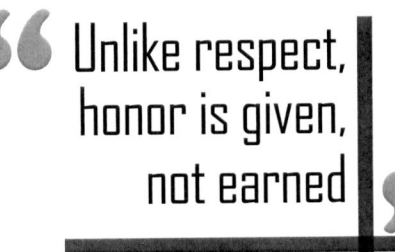

It is the LORD that honors, but He will use other men (and women) to express it. Scriptures speak in Proverbs 8:12 and 18 that; *"I, wisdom, dwell together with prudence; I possess knowledge and discretion; With me are riches and honor, enduring wealth and prosperity (NIV)."* Christ has been made unto us Wisdom (1 Corinthians 1:30), so to have Christ is to receive knowledge, discretion, riches, honor, enduring wealth and prosperity! Honor is sandwiched in-between five other blessings that the LORD bestows on His beloved. *"By humility and the fear of the Lord are riches and honor and life (NKJV),"* says King Solomon in Proverbs 22:4. Humility (of the heart) and reverence for God is the pathway to riches, eternal life and Honor. As we seek God's righteousness (Matthew 6:33) by faith, He promises honor as one of the things that are added to us. Proverbs 21:21 says; *"He who follows righteousness and mercy finds life, righteousness and honor (NKJV)."* Unlike respect, honor is given, not earned

Cultural and Traditional differences and how they influence Honor

"We are, at almost every point of our day, immersed in cultural diversity: faces, clothes, smells, attitudes, values, traditions, behaviors, beliefs, rituals," says Randa Abdel-Fattah.[3]

Each culture has traditional ways it expresses, represents and manifests honor. The way each culture expresses, represents, or manifests honor is determined by their tribe (if any), traditions, beliefs, manners, civilization, exposure, modernity and education.

---

[3]Brainy Quotes: Cultural Diversity Quotes; retrieved from https://www.brainyquote.com/topics/cultural_diversity on 19/09/2018 at 4:15pm

The Advanced English Dictionary (Electronic Version) defines Culture as:

    i) "A particular society at a particular time and place"
    ii) "All the knowledge and values shared by a society"
    iii) "The attitude and behavior that is characteristic of a particular social group or organization."

These definitions specify a few key things; a society in time and space, knowledge and values shared, attitudes, and behaviors. All these cultural factors will determine how a particular group of people will practice honor among themselves. A certain culture should not impose its traditions on other cultures, neither should it judge other cultures for their traditions (as long as those traditions are not demonic, evil, don't abuse human rights, or inflict pain on those who practice them [or are forced into them]). Tradition is defined by the Advanced English Dictionary as:

    i) An inherited pattern of thought or action;
    ii) A specific practice of long standing;
    iii) To transmit by way of tradition;
    iv) To hand down.

Many traditions (patterns of thought, actions, and practices) have been handed down from one generation to another in human societies. Other cultural traditions have died down with time, but for those that have survived civilization and modernity, it is very important to note as Christians that not every cultural tradition is evil, sinful, or demonic, and neither are all cultural traditions holy, uphold human rights and dignity or are in line with biblical sound doctrine.

The Christian, their Culture, and Honor

Bruce Riley Ashford, Jr. is a Professor of Theology and Culture, Dean of Faculty, and Provost at South Eastern Baptist Theological Seminary in North Carolina, USA. In his book, *Every Square Inch: An Introduction to Cultural Engagement for Christians* (Lexham, 2015), Ashford offers three competing views on how we as Christians, interact and engage with culture.

He says:

> One option is to live a life that can be characterized as "Christianity against culture," which views culture as something that a person tries to escape from or fight against. Another option could be called "Christianity of culture," which views culture uncritically as something that can be accepted wholesale into a person's life and church. A final option can be called "Christianity in and for culture," in which a believer seeks to live Christianly within his or her cultural context and for the betterment of that context, while not rejecting it wholesale, on the one hand, or accepting it wholesale, on the other. (Ashford, Bruce Riley. Every Square Inch: An Introduction to Cultural Engagement for Christians (Kindle Locations 172-176. Lexham Press. Kindle Edition).

Being a Christian does not mean fighting against or escaping from culture all together, neither does it mean that we accept every cultural tradition that is thrown at us because we want to remain in touch with our ancestry. Living as a Christian means that we can exist in and for our different cultures, choosing what to accept or reject from culture, yet at the same time representing and pointing people to Christ.

The way Christians practice honor with one another can be influenced by differences in tribe (if any), cultural practices (whether they have evolved overtime or still ancient), beliefs, manners, civilization, exposure, modernity, education, views, perceptions and convictions. An act of honor by a Christian from a different culture might shock the alien, escapist or elitist to that culture, who thinks (either through ignorance about that culture, contempt, or

> **"Living as a Christian means that we can exist in and for our different cultures, choosing what to accept or reject from culture, yet at the same time representing and pointing people to Christ"**

pride) that they are too modern and civilized to do such a thing.

I am born, raised, and live in Africa; and my continent is traditional, tribal and cultural. Each tribe, clan, or family has traditional ways of honor that are different from other tribes, clans, or families. One tribe, clan, or family cannot ridicule, despise, or determine how another honors each other; especially elders. Other than the West and North American modernizations, Africa, Asia and a few countries in Europe still have traditional ways of honoring one another.

Here are some examples;

1) Kneeling: Most tribes in Uganda kneel down for elders.
2) Hugging: Tribes in western Uganda hug one another.
3) Bowing down: The Yoruba of Nigeria, and most tribes in Asia.
4) Kissing on the cheeks: The Tutsi and Hutu of Rwanda, and the French.
5) Prostration: The Baganda tribe in Buganda kingdom in Uganda prostrate before their King, and the Yoruba of Nigeria for their elders.
6) The Basoga in Eastern Uganda lay down on the ground and their king walks on their backs!
7) Other tribes stand on their feet when an elder appears.
8) Feet touching: Most tribes in India do this as a form of honor.
9) Curtsy: In the

> **When people convert to Christianity, sometimes their culture and traditions influence the way they honor their spiritual leaders**

6

UK, this is how royals are greeted, especially the king and queen.

10) In the USA people just shake hands, but also give a standing ovation to a very honorable person.

The above examples show the diverse traditional practices through which different groups of people in Africa and the rest of the world honor each other.

When people convert to Christianity, sometimes their culture and traditions influence the way they honor their spiritual leaders. Since the Bible is a legal and authoritative document for Christianity, discussion of *"Honor in the Gospel"* shall largely be based on the truth found in it.

CHAPTER 2

BUILDING A KINGDOM CULTURE OF HONOR

"The doctrine of the Kingdom of Heaven, which was the main teaching of Jesus, is certainly one of the most revolutionary doctrines that ever stirred and changed human thought." H. G. Wells [4]

A kingdom culture of honor does not just happen by a miracle. It is intentionally cultivated. There can be no honor without understanding how kingdoms operate. Kingdoms are governed by a king. The body of Christ is a Kingdom of its own. God, through Christ Jesus His Son, did not come to earth to start a Fortune-500 company. He came to set up a Kingdom. God is the King of kings and the LORD of Lords, and his sons (male and female) are kings and priests to Him. Kings reign and influence the earth (spheres of religion/faith, family, community, education, leadership and government, the media, arts and entertainment, business and wealth creation). On the other hand, priests minister in the temple (spiritual domains - through worship, prayer, and spiritual gifts). The believer's dual role on earth from heaven's perspective is to be kings and priests.

---

[4] Brainy Quotes; Kingdom Quotes, Retrieved from https://www.brainyquote.com/topics/kingdom on 22/09/2018 at 2:10am

Kings and Priests

Revelation 5:10 says: *"You have made them to be a kingdom and priests to serve our God, and they will reign on the earth (NIV)"* and 1 Peter 2:9 declares that, *"But you are a chosen people, a royal priesthood, a holy nation, a people belonging to God, that you may declare the praises of him who called you out of darkness into his wonderful light (NIV)."*

It is easy to think that we shall only be kings and priests in the millennial reign of Christ. However, Revelation 5:10 has shown us that it starts now. Believers (both Jews and Gentiles) are called out of the world into the Kingdom of God, yet living their normal lives in the world. Furthermore, when we cross reference it with 1 Peter 2:9, scriptures confirm that we are both priests and kings at the same time, here on earth. A royal priesthood means a kingly priest; a Priest (spiritual role) who is a King (physical role). We are kings and priests because of the new priesthood that is of the order of Melchizedek. A king is a king because of his authority exercised through speaking decrees. Kings have authority. God has left the authority over the earth to His body of believers. Some bible teachers refute the suggestion that the Body of Christ should influence (whether directly or indirectly) the different spheres of society. This book's position is the affirmative as I shall elaborate below.

The Ekklesia of God

There is need for an authentic understanding of the true function of the body of Christ on earth as the *Ekklesia*. But what does the word *"Ekklesia"* mean? A small section of Biblical historians, researchers, and scholars think that the New Testament was first written in Aramaic[5] because Jesus and

> **"The believer's dual role on earth from heaven's perspective is to be kings and priests"**

5   Wikipedia: Aramaic Language (18/09/2018); Aramaic Arāmāyā (Hebrew: אֲרָמְרָא, Classical Syriac, Arabic: (ﺍﺭﺍﻣﻴﺔ) is a language or group of languages belonging to the Semitic subfamily of the Afroasiatic

His disciples spoke [and wrote[6]] Aramaic,[7] and not Greek. One of the reasons they give for this thought is that you will find quite a number of Aramaic phrases, words, and nouns in the New Testament[8] that had no direct equivalent of Greek meanings, phrases, or words. Therefore, Greek translators had no choice, but to leave them in Aramaic and interpret their inferred meanings.

With that in mind, let us look at how a direct translation from Aramaic to Greek and to English of Matthew 16:18 should read. But, because I could not find a single scripture that considers all the arguments I have on this particular verse, I will use the *World English Bible Translation*, and expound on it using other words from the *Young's Literal Translation*, *Amplified Bible*, *Complete Jewish Bible*, and other sources[9] from the internet. Matthew 16:18 should read,

> *"I also tell you that you are Peter [Greek; Petros, a piece of a rock or stone], and on this rock [Greek; Petra, a rock mass or bedrock] I will build my assembly [people, community (either scattered or together), congregation assembled together for the purpose of testifying, instructing in a matter of law or to call a witness to testify], and the gates of Hades will not prevail against it."*

The key word I need us to pick out for our discussion and particularly

language family. More specifically, it is part of the Northwest Semitic group, which also includes the Canaanite languages such as Hebrew and Phoenician. (Retrieved from https://en.wikipedia.org/wiki/Aramaic_language on 22/09/2018).

[6] Read more: Archive.Org; Was the New Testament Really Written in Greek? Accessed from https://archive.org/details/WastheNewTestamentReallyWritteninGreek1e on 22/09/2018 at 11:48pm

[7] Wikipedia: Language of Jesus (13/09/2018); It is generally agreed by historians that Jesus and his disciples primarily spoke Aramaic (Jewish Palestinian Aramaic), the common language of Judea in the first century AD, most likely a Galilean dialect distinguishable from that of Jerusalem. The villages of Nazareth and Capernaum in Galilee, where Jesus spent most of his time, were Aramaic-speaking communities. It is also likely that Jesus knew enough Koine Greek to converse with those not native to Palestine, and it is also possible that Jesus knew some Hebrew for religious purposes. (Retrieved from https://en.wikipedia.org/wiki/Language_of_Jesus on 22/09/2018 at 11:58pm)

[8] Aramaic Hebrew New Testament: Aramaic, Retrieved from http://www.hebrewnewtestament.com/aramaic.htm on 25/09/2018 at 8:23pm

[9] John Oakes (October 31, 2008); Did Jesus use the word synagogue or church in Matthew 16:18? Retrieved from http://evidenceforchristianity.org/did-jesus-use-the-word-synagogue-or-church-in-matthew-1618/ on 22/09/2018 at 12:40pm and also Chaim & Laura: Word Study - What is the Church? (March 19, 2015), Retrieved from http://www.chaimbentorah.com/2015/03/word-study-what-is-the-church on 23/09/2018 at 10:34pm

this section is ASSEMBLY/COMMUNITY, because it will help us understand this book's line of thought in a broader sense and how it helps us understand honor. Another fact is that Jesus never used an Aramaic equivalent of the English word "Church " in the New Testament, and neither did the prophets and apostles who wrote the Old and New Testaments. He used one of two possible Aramaic words from which the Greek translators used the word Ekklesia.

So what does the Greek word *Ekklesia* (since it is the exact equivalent of the word Jesus spoke to Peter) mean? Encyclopaedia Britannica describes Ekklesia as a, "gathering of those summoned ", but goes ahead to elaborate that the:

> *"Ekklesia became coterminous with the body of male citizens 18 years of age or over and had final control over policy, including the right to hear appeals in the hēliaia (public court), take part in the election of archons (chief magistrates), and confer special privileges on individuals."*

From the above definition we learn that the Ekklesia was a gathering of those summoned; and this group of people had final control over policy, had the right to hear appeals in the public court, instructed on matters of law, called witnesses to testify, would elect chief magistrates of the city, and also had powers to honor anyone with special privileges. Basically, this Ekklesia was the actual ruling body of a Greek city. It seems that even the chief magistrates of a city relied on the favor and decisions of the Ekklesia, and this same group was like the Court of Appeal for anyone who hadn't been satisfied with the verdict of the magistrates. They also had the power to make anyone anything they wanted (in terms of appointment or elevation). If this is the description and definition of Ekklesia, it is so much different from what we know as Church today!

The Body of Christ is more than just a Sunday gathering in a "church" building. Being accustomed to church buildings has limited our understanding of our true role and position in society; no wonder we have limited influence in our communities and in the world because

12

we are too "inward" minded.

The legal meaning of Ekklesia reveals the authority, power, and influence of God's Kingdom on earth. These kings and priests should have influence and final control over the executive, judicature and legislative spheres in their societies. Society should come to us, not us going to them, because our position is higher than theirs; yet, this is not the case in most countries. I am not in any way advocating for state religions, I am just emphasizing the fact that our influence should go beyond the walls of our "church" buildings and touch every fabric of society.

Describing Kingdom Honor and how it is Cultivated

After understanding that we are kings and priests of an Ekklesia, whose dual role is both in heaven and on earth, it is vital for us to know how kings and priests can live in honor with one another as a king to a king and as a priest to a priest. The result of this will be the healing of broken relationships, minimizing competition and resolving conflicts in leadership and in the Body of Christ.

I have not yet found a scripture that describes Kingdom honor like Joel 2:1-11. We shall read these verses through different versions, highlighting some key points.

> Joel 2: "1 Blow the ram's horn trumpet in Zion! Trumpet the alarm on my holy mountain! Shake the country up! God's Judgment's on its way — the Day's almost here! (The MESSAGE Bible).
>
> 2 A day of darkness and gloominess, A day of clouds and thick darkness,

13

Like the morning clouds spread over the mountains. A people come, great and strong, The like of whom has never been; Nor will there ever be any such after them, Even for many successive generations. 3 "A fire devours before them, And behind them a flame burns; The land is like the Garden of Eden before them, And behind them a desolate wilderness; Surely nothing shall escape them (NKJV)."

4 "Their appearance is like the appearance of horses, and like war horses and horsemen, so do they run (AMP)"

5 "With a noise like chariots Over mountaintops they leap, Like the noise of a flaming fire that devours the stubble, Like a strong people set in battle array (NKJV)."

6 "At the sight of them, nations are in anguish; every face turns pale (NIV).

7 "The invaders charge. They climb barricades. Nothing stops them. Each soldier does what he's told, so disciplined, so determined. 8 They don't get in each other's way. Each one knows his job and does it. Undaunted and fearless, unswerving, unstoppable. 9 They storm the city, swarm its defenses, Loot the houses, breaking down doors, smashing windows. 10 They arrive like an earthquake, sweep through like a tornado. Sun and moon turn out their lights, stars black out (THE MESSAGE Bible)."

11 "And the Lord utters His voice before His army, for His host is very great, and [they are] strong and powerful who execute [God's] word. For the day of the Lord is great and very terrible, and who can endure it? "(AMP).

I have read various commentaries[10] of reputable bible scholars on the above portion of scripture, and because revelation is progressive, there is something else I see in this chapter that none of those commentaries sees. They interpreted it allegorically and futuristically as pertaining to the return of the Lord Jesus Christ and the impending judgement, but I see something different, and it is what I will now discuss.

---

[10]Keil and Delitzsch Commentary on the Old Testament, Bible Knowledge Commentary, The Bible Exposition Commentary: Old Testament, The Biblical Illustrator (Old Testament), and Matthew Henry's Commentary

In Joel 2:1, a trumpet should be blown in Zion because of the coming day of the Lord. My first submission is that Zion and the "holy mountain" represent the Body of Christ on earth, right now.[11] Look at Psalm 87:2-3: *"The Lord loves the gates of Zion more than all the dwellings of Jacob. 3 Glorious things are spoken of you, O city of God! (NKJV)."* Here we see two entities; Zion, and Jacob. Jacob is the nation of Israel, Zion the city and mountain of God is the Ekklesia. He speaks glorious things over the Jews who choose to come from "all the dwelling places of Jacob" and enter the city of God, the same way He does over His body on earth! This is the Ekklesia, for it has all those called out of the dwellings of Jacob and the gentiles from the nations of the earth.

Psalm 102:13,14-16 speaks of the same thing:
> *"You will arise and have compassion on Zion, for it is time to show favor to her; the appointed time has come. 15 The nations will fear the name of the Lord, all the kings of the earth will revere your glory. 16 For the Lord will rebuild Zion and appear in his glory (NIV)."*

Joel 2:1 also speaks of the coming of the Day of the Lord (future). I like the way The Message bible ends verse 1, "the Day's almost here!" Psalm 102:13 declares that the appointed time to show favor to Zion has come, right now. In Psalm 102:15, the nations fear the name of the Lord because of the favor He shows to Zion in the appointed time. That is why Acts 2:5-12 speaks of *Parthians, Medes* and *Elamites*; residents of Mesopotamia, Judea and Cappadocia, Pontus and Asia, Phrygia and Pamphylia, Egypt and the parts of Libya near Cyrene; visitors from Rome (both Jews and converts to Judaism); *Cretans* and *Arabs* as having been amazed when the day of Pentecost "fully came" and the Ekklesia built after the Holy Ghost had been poured out. This "building" is what Psalm 102:16 and Matthew 16:18 speak about; Christ building His Ekklesia.

Psalms 102:16 speaks of "rebuilding" because at that time, Christ was to include the Gentiles in His building (Ephesians 2:19-22), hence "rebuilding". Remember that in Acts 7:38 Stephen, inspired by the Holy Ghost, speaks of the "assembly" in the wilderness (same word –

[11] Further reading; Psalm 132:13-16; 9:14; 48:1-14; Micah 4:6-7; Isaiah 46:13; Hebrews 12:22-24

Ekklesia). When Peter stands up to preach in Acts 2:14-21, he quotes from Joel 2:28-32! The very chapter that has our portion of scripture under scrutiny! Why would commentaries separate verses 1-7 from verses 28-32 as speaking of two different events? Joel chapter 2 is about the Ekklesia; God's Kingdom of kings and priests!

There is another portion of scripture found in Psalm 46:4-5 that says the same thing: *"There is a river whose streams make glad the city of God, the holy place where the Most High dwells. 5 God is within her, she will not fall; God will help her at break of day (NIV)."*

The river spoken about here is the Holy Ghost that Jesus promised the believers. He said he was the river of living water (John 7:37-39). It is the Holy Spirit who makes this Ekklesia glad. The holy place where God dwells is the regenerated spirit of His children, because they are His temple (1 Corinthians 6:19). The God within this temple is "Emmanuel", God with us (Matthew 1:22-23), and we have already talked about the break of Day. The pouring out of the Holy Ghost was the break of the "Day of the Lord". From verses 2 to 3 of Chapter 2, Joel prophecies that the Ekklesia is here, great and strong. Nothing like it had been seen before and nothing like it will ever been seen again, for generations to come. This is the rock that will fill the whole earth, just like Daniel prophesied in (Daniel 2:31-35). It is that cornerstone (Ephesians 2:19-22) that shatters the toes of the image in Nebuchadnezzar's vision. During that time prophesied, no earthly kingdom will escape being devoured by the Ekklesia because it is a formidable force.

These priestly kings are not horses; they just appear as though they are. This is what Joel 2:4 is speaking about. War horses represent strength, training, speed, skill, discipline, submission, order, self-control, and charisma. War horses, because of their training, don't fight each other. They don't compete or outrun each other, rather, they complement and support each other for the common good. Like war horses and horsemen, priestly kings run with the gospel, invading subcultures and societies. They are equipped, skilled, empowered, disciplined, filled with spiritual strength in their inner man (Ephesians 3:16), ready to conquer the kingdoms of this world for their God. Fulfilling that mandate without tearing each other down is an art and discipline of honor.

Joel 2:5 shows how the Ekklesia cannot be hindered by human barriers in the different societies of the earth. They cannot be hindered by language, location, distance, cultural or traditional norms. Nothing can stop the advancement of the gospel. Wherever the Ekklesia goes, every mountain is levelled, and every valley is filled. Have you ever tried to share the gospel with someone only for them to respond with rage and fury? It is not only because you have told them about Jesus, it is because of what is in your spirit that enrages nations and turns the faces of men in anguish against who we are - an Ekklesia. We are different, set apart and called out of the world to be distinct from it.

Joel 2:6 connects well with Psalm 46:6 that says: *"Nations are in uproar, kingdoms fall; he lifts his voice, the earth melts (NIV)."* Nations are in uproar and kingdoms fall because of the existence of the Ekklesia. Some nations restrict religious freedom and pass laws that separate the church from the state as a way of preventing the Ekklesia from being involved in their governance affairs. These nations outlaw Christians while others forbid the clergy from commenting on the politics of the day or stand against injustice. However, during presidential and other political elections, religious leaders are invited to luncheons and dinners, not as influencers, but merely stooges to observe proceedings. This is not honoring the Ekklesia.

The true place of honor for the Ekklesia is when she takes her place as the court of appeal, is part of the leadership of the nation by setting its moral and spiritual agenda, and influences (whether directly or indirectly) the Executive, Legislature, and the Judiciary of that nation. In kingdom honor, the Ekklesia is given her rightful place. Her wisdom and opinion about the moral and spiritual values of a nation are considered. That is kingdom honor. It is not about the leaders of Ekklesia shinning the spotlight on themselves. It is about them helping those they lead to influence their communities.

When that happens and causes positive change, kingdom honor is upheld. Kingdom Honor is the philosophy of discipline of the spirit, determination and conviction of faith. It is understanding one's calling and assignment. It is kingdom-driven and not denominational focused. It is attentive to the voice of God, maintaining one's course, sticking to one's race (vision and grace) and finishing it. These are the keys to honoring God and living in honor with one another. If each of us understood and ran their races faithfully and tried not to interfere with other people's lives, I don't see how we would be threatened if we saw others "succeeding". There would be nothing wrong if we saw both believers and unbelievers flock in large numbers to a particular pastor's church. Instead, we would be happy for them that the Ekklesia is having the impact it should have.

If we understood kingdom honor, we would not get jealous if a ministry that we don't subscribe to had super abundant resources at their disposal. We would be happy that their leaders are traveling the nations and preaching the gospel. We would be glad that they are penetrating the airwaves with their voices, building cathedrals, and whatever things they may choose to do as long as it is for the purpose of the Kingdom. How can we influence communities and spheres of society when we ourselves are thinking like employees of corporate companies; each trying to climb the corporate ladder without minding who we step on or knock down in the process of going up? How can we change communities when we ourselves live in competition with each other (looking at other ministries as competitors, not partners – this

> **Kingdom Honor is the philosophy of discipline of the spirit, determination and conviction of faith. It is understanding one's calling and assignment**

is a corporate mindset, not a kingdom mindset), fight one another, sideline and blackmail each other? Is this honoring one another? If we orchestrate the downfall of other brethren and rejoice when it happens how can we claim to be honorable. Why does a disagreement in doctrine lead to the start of a new denomination (or a new church)? The answer to all these questions and more lies in the lack of a kingdom culture of honor.

If a preacher focused on their preaching, a teacher on their teaching, a worship leader on their ministry, an evangelist on his or her evangelistic campaigns and a business person on their business, we would have less frictions, wars, and conflicts. The media would have less negativity and scorn to write about us. However, the challenge is that we have an opinion on other people's courses. We speak for them as if we have all the facts. We speculate and assume things that they never told us. We sit on the throne of the almighty God and judge other people's motives and strategies, while forgetting our own races. When we do these things, we are not giving them the honor due to them. This ought not to be so.

The Ekklesia of God is an army that invades territories. It is undaunted, fearless, unswerving, unstoppable, relentless and intentional; sweeping through societies like a tornado or a hurricane. As it advances, each of its warriors maintains their courses. Anyone that is part of this army must be acquainted with kingdom honor, which means desisting from breaking the ranks or jostling one another. Instead, each warrior must march straight ahead, maintaining their lane, just like warhorses. War horses don't leave their lanes or shove their way in front of another.

When Prince Harry of the United Kingdom wedded Meghan Markel in London in May of 2018, I was amazed to see paired horses marching seamlessly. They brought out the meaning of Joel 2:7 so well. These horses kept their course, effortlessly marching straight forward without trying to outcompete each other. They complemented each other, neither moving too fast nor too slow. They respected the ranks and honored one another. These horses were decent, sticking to their role to the dot because they are trained for royalty. This is the attitude that kingly priests should have. An attitude of royalty, respect and honor.

The great commission as presented in Mathew 28:19 was not about the Ekklesia sitting, standing, thinking, resting or planning to go, but an actual getting up and going. Once we start to go, nothing can stop us. However, as long as we are building monuments for ourselves while pushing, shoving and back-stabbing one another, we will continue to experience frictions, factions, and conflicts in the body of Christ. This is not kingdom honor that kings and priests ought to cultivate. Kingdom honor releases and sends men into their own courses. If leaders in the body of Christ followed the "owners" manual and sent men into the world to make disciples of all nations, we would have less "church" splits. The Ekklesia has been expanding because men were sent (either willingly or unwillingly). If we choose to go into all the world and expand the kingdom of our God while honoring Him, ourselves and others, He will go before us, preparing the way for those who obey and execute His word.

In writing this book, I am not, in any way, advocating for titles or positions because even as kingly priests, we ought to live with the attitude of honor defined by "Servant Leaders"[12] and not dictatorial despots. However, to better understand kingdom honor, we need to know how a typical monarchy[13] looks like. The UK's House of Windsor is a perfect example of a monarchy,[14] albeit not a traditional one like those in medieval times, but a constitutional monarchy. A monarchy has the following characteristics and roles:[15]

---

[12]"The servant-leader is servant first.... It begins with the natural feeling that one wants to serve, to serve first." - Robert K. Greenleaf. From his book; Servant Leadership: A Journey into the Nature of Legitimate Power and Greatness, Paulist Press, 1977

[13]Wikipedia: Monarchy (21/09/2018); A monarchy is a form of government in which a group, generally a family representing a dynasty (aristocracy), embodies the country's national identity and its head, the monarch, exercises the role of sovereignty. Retrieved from https://en.wikipedia.org/wiki/Monarchy on 26/09/2018 at 11:29pm

[14]The home of the Royal Family: Retrieved from https://www.royal.uk/ on 27/09/2018 at 12:12am

[15]The Home of the Royal Family: The Role of The Monarchy; Retrieved from https://www.royal.uk/role-monarchy on 27/09/2018 at 2:21am

> **"The believer's dual role on earth from heaven's perspective is to be kings and priests"**

20

1) Royal titles, ranks and the nobility: In kingdoms, royal roles are explicitly defined by one's title, rank and nobility. Each holder of a title, rank or nobility learns the culture and honor surrounding their title, rank or nobility and honors other holders of the same with the honor that is due to them.

2) A king is head of state: In constitutional monarchies, this position is more formal and ceremonial than political, but still plays an important role in the kingdom. It has significant influence on the constitutional government, political affairs, social life and the stability of the state. The reigning king or queen takes on some constitutional and representational duties.

3) A king or queen (in the case of the House of Windsor) is the identity of the kingdom, the uniting factor, the inspiration of patriotism and voluntarism. He or she is a symbol of continuity.

4) A king or queen opens new sessions of the council of lords (parliament), grants assent to legislations (this means that these legislations have to be in their favor, not against) and approves orders and proclamations.

5) A king or queen retains the right to appoint and dismiss the prime minister who serves the interests of the monarchy.

6) Through his or her generosity, a king or queen supports and encourages hard work, achievement, innovation, ingenuity, chivalry, selflessness, service, loyalty, bravery, sacrifice and philanthropy. He or she does this through awarding titles, honors, gifts (land, silver, gold, medals, certificates, etc.) and invitations to parties, receptions and celebrations.

7) A king or queen is a figure of the creation, passing, enforcement and maintenance of law and the establishment of the legal systems of a kingdom.

8) When meeting a king or queen, courtesy and tradition; not obligatory codes of behavior, determine how he or she should be greeted. In the UK[16] for instance, the traditional way men greet the Queen is by a neck bow (from head only), while women do a simple curtsy.[17]

9) A king or queen is the foremost representative of the kingdom's military army, holding its supreme rank.

10) In the UK[18], the queen holds the title of 'Defender of the Faith'; which means that she fights, defends, upholds and 'protects' the Church of England against any evil onslaughts. She also appoints Archbishops, Bishops and Deans of the Church of England.

Even though worldly kingdoms are in no way a parallel to the Kingdom of heaven on earth, the example of the House of Windsor gives us a snapshot of the role of the Ekklesia in influencing the affairs of nations on the earth and its mandate in shaping culture, policy, laws, governance, and livelihoods, among others. They also show us the church's divine purpose to bring heaven on earth. It has a culture of honor and generosity. One of its responsibilities is to guide nations into doing what it right. The above characteristics also show us the church's nobility in the way it represents the King of Kings, and its greatness in comparison to political governments in this world.

---

[16] The Home of the Royal Family: The Role of The Monarchy; Retrieved from https://www.royal.uk/role-monarchy on 27/09/2018 at 2:21am

[17] Wikipedia: Curtsey (21/09/2018); A curtsey (also spelled curtsy, courtesy in British English, or incorrectly as courtsey) is a traditional gesture of greeting, in which a girl or woman bends her knees while bowing her head. It is the female equivalent of male bowing or genuflecting in Western cultures. Retrieved from https://en.wikipedia.org/wiki/Curtsey on 27/09/2018 at 1:46am

[18] The Home of the Royal Family: The Role of The Monarchy; Retrieved from https://www.royal.uk/role-monarchy on 27/09/2018 at 2:21am

If all of us related with one another in honor as earthly royals do, human relationships in the body of Christ would be much better than they are now. Using the examples of the roles and characteristics of a monarchy that we just looked at and the scriptural reference we have discussed so far, this is how kingdom honor for every kingly priest would look like:

1) Understanding your personal mandate and assignment by trying not to be like someone else. No one else on earth has your finger prints and DNA makeup! Be who God created you to be.

2) Running your race, at your own pace and finishing it well like Paul (in 2 Timothy 4:7-8) says: *"I have fought the good fight, I have finished the race, I have kept the faith (NKJV)."* The story of two men, the Cushite and a one Ahimaaz in 2 Samuel 28:1-32 is a good lesson on running at your own pace. Ahimaaz was a swift runner, to the point of even outrunning the Cushite, yet he did not have the tidings concerning the death of Absalom. The Cushite on the other hand, though a slow runner, carried the tidings because "the race is not to the swift... (Ecclesiastes 9:11)."

3) Standing firm in the calling in which you have been called, and remaining in the grace and measure of faith you have been given.

4) Watching against the spirit of judgement, for *"Who are you to judge another's servant? To his own master he stands or falls. Indeed, he will be made to stand, for God is able to make him stand (Romans 14:4 NKJV)."*

> **If all of us related with one another in honor as earthly royals do, human relationships in the body of Christ would be much better than they are now**

5) Some ministers of the gospel will choose to go by their "offices" (Apostle, Prophet, Evangelist, Pastor, and Teacher), whereas others will choose to be referred to by their first names, or nicknames. Against such there are no rules, regulations, or laws. Whether it is first name or "office", that is all up to the individual. Interestingly, Paul, in almost all his letters, introduced himself as "Paul, an Apostle of Jesus Christ..." Why should one man's liberty be judged by another man's conscience? Remember what we said about judging in point four above?

6) Kingdom honor allows the wheat and the tares to grow together because if one tries to weed out the tares, they might accidentally also weed out the wheat because they are identical. And remember that it is not your garden, but the Master's (Selah).

> **A person who learns to see and know nothing in people except Christ crucified is a true man/woman of honor; trained in the spirit, mature in the faith, grounded in grace and abounding in love. Such an individual has obtained a high rank in the army of God**

7) Giving other people the same grace that you also constantly need because we all have an "evil day" to deal with someday.

8) Understanding that excellence and high standards do not mean pride. Some people just choose to have unlimited faith and decide to believe God for the whole world. In the aftermath, what manifests as extravagance

and pride are just glimpses of what they believed God for and the standards they have set for themselves.

9)Knowing that someone's place of faith might be another man's place of temptation. This means that the things that scare some, like thinking they will sin because of abundance and greatness, are a fulfilment of faith to others. Both men stand on different footings. Honor those whose manifestation of their grace and faith is different from yours.

10) Understanding that what we criticize today, might appeal to us tomorrow, if we are given the same opportunities or challenges. Give people the grace you will need from them some day!

11. Seeing the gold in the dross! *"Therefore, from now on, we regard no one according to the flesh… (2 Corinthians 5:16, NKJV)."* This is one of the hardest spiritual disciplines. A person who learns to see and know nothing in people except Christ crucified is a true man or woman of honor; trained in the spirit, mature in the faith, grounded in grace and abounding in love. Such an individual has obtained a high rank in the army of God.

- -

"A kingdom is the governing influence of a king over his territory, impacting it with his personal will, purpose and intent, producing a culture, values, morals, and lifestyle that reflect the king's desires and nature for his citizens." [19]

"As citizens of Heaven, we inhabit the earth for the purpose of influencing it with the culture and values of heaven and bringing it under the government of the King of Heaven." [20]

- -

[19]Munroe, Myles; Kingdom Principles, Lulu Enterprises Incorporated, 2013
[20]ibid

CHAPTER 3

HONOR, SPIRITUAL LEADERSHIP AND HUMILITY

"When he had finished washing their feet, he put on his clothes and returned to his place. "Do you understand what I have done for you?" he asked them. 13 "You call me 'Teacher' and 'Lord,' and rightly so, for that is what I am. 14 Now that I, your Lord and Teacher, have washed your feet, you also should wash one another's feet. 15 I have set you an example that you should do as I have done for you. 16 I tell you the truth, no servant is greater than his master, nor is a messenger greater than the one who sent him. 17 Now that you know these things, you will be blessed if you do them." [21]

It is very easy for those in leadership, because of the perks that come with their "positions", to take those they lead for granted. Christ, the greatest leader that ever lived, demonstrated that true leadership is through humility and not superiority.

Leading through humility is honor to those we lead. As leaders, we should never think of ourselves as greater than those we lead.

---

21 Christ Jesus; John 13:12-17, New International Version

Humility and Servant Leadership; the mark of true spiritual leadership

Over the years, the church has taught about "Spiritual Authority and Submission". These teachings emphasize obedience from those being led towards those in leadership. However, such teachings largely miss out the important aspect that should show "how leaders relate with their followers". This imbalance has resulted in the abuse of leadership, violation of people's inherent need for honor, abuse of relationships and the creation of master-slave attitudes and tendencies. This has led to the misuse of resources, spiritual manipulation, dependence on men of God rather than on God, resulting in the creation of "demi-gods" who live extravagant and self-indulgent lifestyles. The Ekklesia has ended up with ministers of God becoming untouchables, while believers have become "second class citizens" or more like slaves.

Honor, on the other hand, is a trait of kingdom living that goes beyond spiritual authority and submission and encompasses those in leadership and those under leadership to enrich each other holistically. Honor is about mutual relationships through respect. It is about living

> ❝ Honor is about mutual relationships through respect. It is about living in peace and harmony with those in leadership and those being led ❞

in peace and harmony with those in leadership and those being led, thinking less of ourselves while esteeming others more than ourselves. Honor is the true mark of spiritual leadership because everybody is included.

Before servant leaders can be recognized or held in high regard, they should not demand honor, recognition, or regard in any way. It is false leaders who crave to be honored. A hierarchical kind of leadership loads it over the people, just like the Pharisees did. The sons of Zebedee (Mark 10:35-45) pestered Jesus to give them high-ranking positions in His kingdom. However, Jesus told them that He had not come to bring that kind of leadership that loads it over those who are being led. Jesus told them that He had brought servant leadership. A servant leader does not seek honor. God gives it to them. To be secure as a leader means that one has no self-seeking motives. Self-serving leaders are a great snare and liability to Christian leadership.

> "Jesus Christ modeled spiritual leadership in a perfect way, not only through the words that He spoke, but also through His character"

Egotism is the enemy of servant leadership. Jesus came to serve, not to be served. Paul speaks of the mind which was in Christ (Philippians 2:5-11); which in essence is a servant-hood mentality; a mindset that seeks to serve others, a mind that does not consider itself of its own interests, but that looks out for the interest of others. The art of spiritual leadership is displayed all over the pages of Scripture.

Spiritual leadership, as defined by J. Oswald Sanders in his book[22], "Spiritual Leadership", is a 'matter of being chosen, rather than choosing, all about being last, rather than first.'" From this definition, we learn that spiritual leadership is not given to one by merit, but by God's sovereign grace and purpose. It is a privilege and honor to be called into the ministry. However, many in Christian leadership behave like they are doing God's people a favor by leading them.

[22]Spiritual Leadership: A Commitment to Excellence for Every Believer, Moody Publishers, 2007

It is only God who is indispensable, irreplaceable and infallible; all of us are dispensable, replaceable and fallible. We should, therefore, minister with a servant-leadership mentality. Jesus Christ modeled spiritual leadership in a perfect way, not only through the words that He spoke, but also through His character. He was a servant-leader who went as far as washing his disciples' feet. J. Oswald Sanders continues to say that, "Servant leadership is the aim of spiritual leadership."[23] That is to say, our motive in becoming spiritual leaders should be to serve, not to be served. Sadly, professionalizing the gospel by standing behind the pulpit has subtly led us (mostly church leaders) to unconsciously think of ourselves as meritorious.

The gospel is more than the forty minutes we stand before people preaching. The most effective way to preach is to live the gospel through our day–to-day mundane activities. Like my friends at Worship Harvest Ministries in Kampala, Uganda say: "Church Begins on Monday." Our light shines more if put in the dark world, rather than hiding it in the four walls of our churches.

In teaching about servant leadership, Jesus in Matthew 23:11-12, said: *"But he who is greatest among you shall be your servant. 12 And whoever exalts himself will be humbled, and he who humbles himself will be exalted NKJV."* That scriptures ties well into 1 Corinthians 4:9 where Paul also says, *"For it seems to me that God has put us apostles on display at the end of the procession…….NIV."* When Apostle Wayne Lee Jnr, a man of God from Jasper - Alabama, USA, showed me this scripture, it blew me away. He said that if leadership is like a procession, church leaders are at the end of the line, not at the front. Those in spiritual leadership should be the servants of all. They must lead from behind, equipping and empowering the weak. They must raise next-generation leaders, sending those they lead forward into their destinies and making disciples of nations. We must know that God abhors self-exaltation and pride. He says He "resists the proud" by allowing situations and circumstances to "clip their wings". What J. Oswald Sanders says is also true on this point, "Arrogance undermines a leader's ministry and effectiveness and causes him to lose favor with both the flock and the Lord. God will give

---

[23] ibid

30

power to the humble leader."[24]

Someone posted a picture in a WhatsApp group of a leadership school I attended while writing this book. This picture had a pack of wolves headed in a certain direction. The first three in the procession were old and sick wolves. These gave the rest of the pack its pace. The next five were the strongest, those at the frontline, the fighters. In the center of the procession was the rest of the pack followed by another set of five; the strong fighter wolves. Last of them all, alone, at the end of the pack, was the real leader. He was the Alpha who controlled everything from the rear, having the ability to see all the pack and everything around them, and to make decisions on their direction. True spiritual leadership can be compared to a pack of wolves. The real leader should be the servant of them all; leading from the end of the procession, seeing the needs and circumstance of everyone in the pack. He should monitor the progress of the pack using the skill of maximum emotional intelligence, providing physical, emotional, and social support to the team. As he does this, he should raise new leaders from the pack.

Even in the natural realm, the greatest leaders of all time have been the servants of all. Take Martin Luther King Jr, Mother Theresa and Nelson Mandela as examples. They were selfless, sacrificial, bold and with strong convictions. They sought the good of others, inspiring hope and speaking out against injustice. They were willing to die for the sake of others. Their influence can never be erased. It will continue to live on for many generations to come.

Biblical Representations of Recognizing Servant Leaders

A powerful quote in J. Oswald Sanders book goes: *"Often the crowd does not recognize a leader until he has gone, and then they build a monument for him with the stones they threw at him in life."* [25] Even if those in leadership are supposed to be the servants of all, we are admonished, either in

---

[24]Spiritual Leadership: A Commitment to Excellence for Every Believer, Moody Publishers, 2007, pg. 49
[25]ibid.

representation, manifestation or expression, to recognize those that the Lord has set before us. The kingdom of God is a kingdom of order and not chaos. God established spiritual leaders because He is the ultimate leader who leads through His sons (male and female) to execute His authority and influence on the earth. It is God who gave some the responsibility of urging and guiding others in obedience to the Lordship of Christ. As we obey the Lordship of Christ, we will bring everything and everyone on earth to be subject under His Lordship.

However, we cannot extend this Lordship or bring everything and everyone under His Lordship if we ourselves do not honor those that He has set before us as representations of His Lordship. The Holy Spirit, through the Apostle Paul, urges us to "overwhelm" those that the Lord has set before us with appreciation and love! This is what the verse says:

> *"And now, friends, we ask you to honor those leaders who work so hard for you, who have been given the responsibility of urging and guiding you along in your obedience. 13 Overwhelm them with appreciation and love! Get along among yourselves, each of you doing your part"* (1 Thessalonians 5:12-13).

How do you overwhelm someone with appreciation and love? First of all, it depends on whether you receive and recognize them as your spiritual leader and secondly, you determine how you want to overwhelm them with appreciation and love. There is no law, restrictions, or set boundaries as to how far you can go with this. You can choose what you think will most express appreciation and love and thereby overwhelm them with that.

> *1 Kings 2:19: "Bathsheba went to King Solomon to present Adonijah's request. The king got up and welcomed her, bowing respectfully, and returned to his throne. Then he had a throne put in place for his mother, and she sat at his right hand." (NKJV)*

King Solomon, who was great in wisdom, power, riches and glory, chose to honor his mother. First of all, when she went before his throne, he got up on his feet and welcomed her. He then bowed respectfully to her because he recognized the position she held in his life. He invited her to sit at his right hand, and on a throne he provided. He not only honored her because she was his mother, but also because she had a political position in the kingdom; that of a queen mother. King Solomon understood kingdom honor, protocol and order.

> *1 Kings 18:7: "Now as Obadiah was on his way, suddenly Elijah met him; and he recognized him, and fell on his face, and said, "Is that you, my lord Elijah?" (NKJV)*
> *2 Kings 2:15: "Now when the sons of the prophets who were from Jericho saw him, they said, "The spirit of Elijah rests on Elisha." And they came to meet him, and bowed to the ground before him (NKJV)."*

In 1 Kings 18:3 we read that Obadiah feared the LORD greatly (NKJV), yet when he met Elijah in verse 7 and recognized him, he fell on his face and called him *his* lord. Obadiah feared the LORD, but he also honored the man through whom the LORD worked. When we recognize the Spirit upon a man, we honor that Spirit; not the man himself, but the Spirit on him and the anointing he possesses. Recognizing those the LORD has set before us is one way of honoring Him.

In the book of 2 Kings 2, we read about how Elijah was taken to heaven by a chariot of fire and Elisha, his spiritual son, received a double portion of his spirit. In the midst of all this activity was what the Bible calls the "sons of the prophets" or "a company of prophets" (presumably, a training school for upcoming prophets) who watched all this take place.

When the sons of the prophets saw that the spirit of Elijah rested on Elisha, they approached him, submitted themselves to his service and bowed to the ground. It seems like Elijah and later Elisha were prophets of a higher rank among this company of prophets. They were of a higher position and authority before whom other prophets submitted. Like Apostle Grace Lubega of Phaneroo Ministries in Kampala-Uganda says: *"All those in spiritual callings and offices are ranked."* Understanding another minister's spiritual rank will help us deal with them honorably as those that God has set before us. It does not matter how anointed or called each of us might be, there is always someone we can honor and submit to. When we meet such people, we cannot choose not to give them the honor that is due to them.

> *Exodus 18:7-8: "So Moses went out to meet his father-in-law, bowed down, and kissed him. And they asked each other about their well-being, and they went into the tent (NKJV)."*

> *1 Samuel 24:8: David also arose afterward, went out of the cave, and called out to Saul, saying, "My lord the king!" And when Saul looked behind him, David stooped with his face to the earth, and bowed down (NKJV)."*

Moses was one of the greatest prophets to have ever lived. However, when his father-in-law (who was also his "spiritual father") came to see him, he bowed down and kissed him because he honored him as his father. The prophet Samuel anointed David as the king who was to replace Saul. However, even with this knowledge, David recognized Saul's position as the "sitting" king. He did not dishonor his lord and king. No wonder scripture calls him a man after God's own heart.

Honoring another man does not mean that you are lowering yourself beneath them, it just means that you recognize the spiritual position they hold in your life, the anointing upon their lives, the Spirit they operate in and that you prefer and esteem them above yourself. Understanding spiritual relationships is very pivotal in growing in honor.

- -

"For you know that we dealt with each of you as a father deals with his own children, 12 encouraging, comforting and urging you to live lives worthy of God, who calls you into his kingdom and glory." [26]

- -

---
26 1Thessalonians. 2:11-12, New International Version

CHAPTER 4

HONOR IN SPIRITUAL RELATIONSHIPS

"Elisha saw this and cried out, "My father, my father, the chariots of Israel and its horsemen!" And he saw Elijah no more! Then he took hold of his own clothes and tore them in two pieces." [27]

Many years ago, a certain man of God opened up to me about his spiritual father's failures. Whether what he said was true or not, telling me about them was wrong. Before that, my conscience and attitude towards the man of God who was talked about was very pure. However, after learning of his personal sins, I battled for years to still look at him with a clear and pure conscience void of offence and not regard him after the flesh.

- -

Between 1998 and 2005, a very young man at that time, who is now Apostle Henry Wynn Kakooza of Vast Grace Missions in Gayaza - Uganda, chose to honor and serve his spiritual father in doing menial tasks.

He carried his bag, delivered his letters on foot for conferences and escorted him to different kinds of meetings. He organized his office, <u>ran back and forth</u> to his home to pick or drop off stuff. Henry wrote

[27] 2 Kings 2:12, New King James Version

and read his spiritual father's emails, brushed his shoes and did anything and everything that his "soldier-like" spiritual father instructed him to do. He did it with gladness of heart. Those menial tasks were besides the church-related activities this young man did in his spiritual father's church. He waited on pastors and washed their hands at meal time during conferences. He interpreted sermons for non-English speakers and cleaned the church. He cleaned the toilet, participated in evangelism and was an active member of the prayer ministries.

He played local African drums during praise and worship sessions. In the process of serving his spiritual father, a door opened for him to travel and live in the USA for close to four years. He returned to Uganda, married a beautiful daughter of a great man of God in his country and started a thriving church-planting ministry that has established 54 churches across Uganda and South Sudan. This young man is a true depiction of what honor through spiritual relationships is about.

- -

One of the reasons why people honor one another (mostly their spiritual leaders) is the aspect of spiritual parenting. It is impossible to separate honor from spiritual relationships; that is why understanding these relationships is important and a significant key in appreciating honor.

Advocating for Spiritual Relationships

The term "spiritual fathers" is one of the most highly debatable, despised, criticized, and rejected term (or doctrine) in the body of Christ because of the following arguments of scripture:

1) Matthew 23:9: "And do not call anyone on earth 'father,' for you have one Father, and he is in heaven (NIV)." Opponents use this verse to assert that no one should be a spiritual father to anyone because all of us are children of God, our Father in heaven.

2) Revelation 5:10: "And have made us kings and priests to our God; And we shall reign on the earth (NKJV)." Furthermore, they emphasize that because we are all kings and priests to our God, our relationship is directly to

Him, therefore, we don't need any spiritual father. In response to the two scriptures above and many more like them, I submit the following thoughts and arguments:

1) The book of Matthew chapter 23 where the first scripture is quoted from is, in context, about Jesus' rebuttal at the Teachers of the Law and the Pharisees, who, among other evils, did not practice what they preached. Hypocrites; Jesus called them. Jesus referred to them thus partly because their worth came from seeking recognition and honor from men. They loved attention, always wanting to be greeted (first) and for men to call them "Rabbi" in public places. These men were show offs and egoistic, only desiring to be seen by men!

Therefore, in verse nine, Jesus advises His disciples and the crowd that had gathered to hear Him teach, not to seek honor or wish to be called "father" in a manner like the Pharisees did. Jesus was extremely angry at the Pharisees, to the extent that the NIV version of the bible records seven "woe to you" phrases directed to the teachers of the law and the Pharisees for all their evil and hypocrisy. (Biblical numerology teachers teach that seven is the number of completion; therefore, Christ completed his judgement upon them). It is the Pharisees' and Teachers of the Law's pride and hypocrisy that Jesus was against.

2) I concur that we are all indeed kings and priests unto our God as Revelation 5:10 says. However, we cannot read that verse in isolation, rejection, or ignorance of multiple other scriptures[28] from both the Old and the New Testaments about spiritual fathers and spiritual sons. It is also true that we cannot find a complete book or chapter in the Bible focusing on this topic alone. However, is not most of Christian theology built on different scriptures for a particular theme scattered in different places of the written word of God?

---

[28]Read more; Genesis 45:8; 2 Kings 2:12; 2 Timothy 1:2; Titus 1:4; Philippians 2:19-22; 1 Peter 2:2; 1 John 2:1; and 1 Thessalonians 2:11-12, among others

Understanding Spiritual Relationships

"I am not writing this to shame you, but to warn you, as my dear children. 15 Even though you have ten thousand guardians in Christ, you do not have many fathers, for in Christ Jesus I became your father through the gospel. 16 Therefore I urge you to imitate me. 17 For this reason I am sending to you Timothy, my son whom I love, who is faithful in the Lord. He will remind you of my way of life in Christ Jesus, which agrees with what I teach everywhere in every church." [29]

1 Corinthians 4:14-17 is a good place to start our next discussion. First of all, Paul writes to the Corinthians and calls them his dear children because he loved them (even though he had not given birth to them biologically). Secondly, he alludes to the fact that they have ten thousand guardians, instructors and teachers in Christ (meaning that they could learn from so many), but says they did not have many fathers. In 2010, one of my spiritual mentors; Apostle Rick Clendenen from Kentucky, USA, was the first person to show me that Paul did not say that we cannot have more than one spiritual father (as it is commonly believed or taught), but that he said that we do not have many. This means that we can have more than one, but not many.

> **The way Paul refers to Timothy as his beloved son is different from the way he refers to the Corinthians as dear children. A son (male and female) is one who has matured in relationship with his father**

Thirdly, Paul told the Corinthians that he had become their father through the gospel. This means that they became his spiritual children when they believed the gospel through his preaching. Next,

---

[29] Paul of Tarsus, 1 Corinthians 4:14-17, NIV

he asked them to imitate him; to do what he did - become spiritual fathers to other people through the preaching of the gospel. And then he recommended Timothy to them; his son whom he loved, who was faithful in the Lord, knew Paul's way of life in Christ and agreed with what Paul taught in every assembly of believers. From that portion of scripture, we learn a few things:

>  **Spiritual Fathers believe in their sons and call out their true identity. They see them for who they truly are**

i) We "automatically" become spiritual fathers when we win anyone to Christ. Paul likens that process to "birth pangs" in Galatians 4:19. This, though, does not necessarily mean that we will also raise them in the Lord, nor does it mean that a pastor of a local assembly is automatically its spiritual father. Spiritual fatherhood is more effective and beneficial when it is practiced on individual basis, not with the masses. The way Paul refers to Timothy as his beloved son is different from the way he refers to the Corinthians as dear children. A son (male and female) is one who has matured in relationship with his father.

ii) Love and commitment are the binding codes of this relationship. A spiritual father should love and be committed to raising you in the Lord. If they are not committed to you, the relationship cannot be sustained. You, on the other hand, ought to pursue this relationship if you want to see it grow. There has to be intentionality on both ends of the relationship.

iii)We can learn from many teachers, instructors and guardians, even as many as ten thousand. *"We should always aim to read something different; not only the writers with whom we agree, but those with whom we are ready to do battle. Their point of view challenges us to examine the truth and to test their views. Don't be afraid of new ideas,"* says Muriel Ormrod.[30] The Internet has brought thousands of bible teachers, instructors, and guardians close to us, many of whom we may never meet. However, we can learn from them through their materials. Read, study and learn as much as you can.

iv) We can have more than one spiritual father, but not many. I think that there is a spiritual father for every level of spiritual growth. A spiritual growth assessment would help in determining what kind of spiritual father you need at a particular spiritual growth stage of your life.

v) Not every spiritual father is ready and prepared to take on the role of fathering you in the gospel. Maybe their role was to just give birth to you in the gospel, but another father's role is to raise you in the faith. Find that man or woman who is willing to take you on in their arms.

vi) When we are fully mature in the faith (regardless of physical age), we produce spiritual children after our own kind through the gospel. Some will stay, but others will stray into other men's spiritual parentage.

vii) True spiritual sons are faithful and loyal both to the Lord, and to their spiritual fathers. They possess their spiritual father's DNA and also understand their spirit, way of life, doctrine, convictions, reactions, what they would say in a given situation, unspoken words, strengths and weaknesses, what they love, their desires, purpose, faith, dreams and vision.[31] Paul was confident that Timothy could represent him fully to the Corinthians, as if he himself was there with them.

---

[30] J. Oswald Sanders; Spiritual Leadership: A Commitment to Excellence for Every Believer, Moody Publishers, 2007
[31] 2 Timothy 3:10-11

viii) I wish to submit a personal conviction that a spiritual father can either be male or female. The same way sons of God are male and female. There is no need to call female spiritual leaders "spiritual mothers". This also applies to female prophets that gender-sensitive people call prophetesses. There is neither male nor female before God,[32] and spiritual gifts are also neither male or female.

How Spiritual Fathers Honor their Spiritual Sons

I need to emphasize again that spiritual fatherhood and sonship is relational in nature and not based on any legal requirements or obligations. This means that there has to be a spiritual connection, freedom and willingness between a spiritual father and a son. There also has to be a certain kind of agreement between their spirits, because every seed-bearing tree produces after its own kind. To guard ourselves against error, misuse, manipulation and abuse of spiritual relationships, let us look at the nature and roles of a spiritual father to their spiritual sons (so that those who choose to honor other people as their spiritual fathers know what they should expect):

1) Spiritual Fathers believe in their sons and call out their true identity. They see them for who they truly are. They show them the kingdom and their destiny, and how they fit into it. My spiritual father was the first person to recognize the apostolic call upon my life. He actually began calling me "Apostle" in my early 20s. By that time, the many gifts I possessed and manifested had me confused about who I was in the Kingdom. He saw this and called it forth, then I began to pursue and walk in it. By "calling out my 'calling'" at an early age, he was honoring me. He was not afraid that I would grow, supersede him and take over his ministry. I honor him for defining my spiritual identity and place in the Kingdom.

2) Spiritual fathers nurture, build, raise, rebuke, correct, affirm and encourage. My spiritual father, Bishop Solomon Mukonjo of Church of God in Kamwokya in Kampala, Uganda, did these things and more as he raised me in the faith. On the flip side of this, if a spiritual son is not willing to receive from the spiritual father,

---

[32] Galatians 3:28

the relationship cannot be beneficial to either of them. Honouring spiritual relationships is when a spiritual father gives of himself and a spiritual son is willing to receive from him.

3) Spiritual parents offer wisdom, knowledge, counsel, advice and answers to complex spiritual questions in life. They are humble enough to help us work through stressing issues. They walk with us through life's physical and spiritual storms. When my biological mother died, my spiritual father was a very great encouragement to my siblings and I as we went through those trying years of our lives. He and his wife actually "unofficially" adopted my brother and I into their family.

4) They leave an inheritance for their children's children (Proverbs 13:22). This inheritance is spiritual, physical, emotional, relational, intellectual and financial in nature. An effective spiritual father has to think generational, way past his own lifespan into the generations of his great-grandchildren and plan an inheritance for them. Some of the struggles we go through as we mature are a result of fathers (whether physical or spiritual) who failed to plan past their generations.

I met a wonderful man of God who had transitioned into a ministry after his pastor friend had passed on. Unfortunately, besides the congregation being really small, the new pastor also inherited outstanding debts left by the man of God for the small church to pay. This new pastor had never even been in that ministry. The deceased pastor had not raised any spiritual sons. Sadly, the biggest debt did not even come from anything the pastor had done that was related to the church, but personal activities, while the lesser debt (another big amount) had procured something for the church that they really did not need. This point is very important and sensitive for those who strive to raise spiritual sons. We must honor them with an inheritance. As we raise sons, we ought to ask questions like, "What can they inherit from us?" Is a spiritual inheritance (what is deposited in them) the only legacy we leave for them? Don't we need to prepare for our spiritual children the same way we prepare for our biological ones? Some people think that a spiritual inheritance is all that matters, but I disagree. Besides a spiritual deposit (which is fundamental and key, without which all others are useless), spiritual children also need divine relationships, contacts and connections, education and employment opportunities, vibrant, strong and healthy ministries (regardless of the size) and income-generating projects from their spiritual fathers.

> **Besides a spiritual deposit, spiritual children also need divine relationships, contacts and connections**

5) They help us to see spiritual truths that had been hidden from us for years and they deposit spiritual wealth in us. I thank God because I sat under a thorough teacher of the word as my pastor for over 25 years. We were introduced to Greek interpretation of scripture at a very early age. My spiritual father opened our spiritual eyes to the wealth that is embedded in the Word. He expounded scriptures to us so that we all understood them. It is very rare to hear a sermon today that my pastor never hinted on in some way or the other years ago. That is how "deep" he was and still is.

6) Spiritual fathers should be the direct representation of God the Father's heart, the true image of a husband, a father, a mother and a wife to those who look up to them. John Maxwell says that character is caught, not taught. An effective spiritual father is the model of the heart of God, full of love, compassion and generosity. From them, we learn how to be husbands, fathers and wives. I have not yet met a loving, forgiving and faithful pastor, husband and father like my spiritual father, Bishop Solomon Mukonjo (Church of God

Kamwokya in Kampala, Uganda). Faithfulness, integrity, honesty, unconditional love, forgiveness and humility are the true marks of a spiritual father. My spiritual father has depicted these qualities over the years.

7) Spiritual fathers are consistent. They should not waver or be moved by every form of doctrine. They should be grounded, unfaltering and steady in the word.

8) Spiritual fathers reconcile their spiritual sons to previous relationships that went bad. The book of Philemon is a great example of this. Paul honorably reconciled Onesimus' relationship with his former boss, Philemon. Both Philemon and Onesimus were Paul's spiritual sons. That's what spiritual fathers do.

9) A true spiritual father gives his spiritual sons direct access whenever they need him. They don't have to go through protocol to get to their spiritual fathers because there is an open door of communication for them.

10) Spiritual fathers cannot become biological fathers. Each father has their role, but a biological father can be a spiritual father if they know the Lord and can play both roles. Actually, if your biological father is your spiritual father the better because they know you better than anyone else. Sadly, very few men can play these two roles at the same time.

11) They create a safe environment for innovation, experimentation, demonstration, feedback, failure and growth in the things of God. Besides leading worship and interpreting sermons, my spiritual father also allowed us to preach at a very young age. After the service, he would sit with us and offer feedback and advice on how we could preach better. He would send us to preach in his place in places where he couldn't go. When we erred in the Word, he corrected us in love and expounded the scriptures again to us. With this man of God, a simple question would turn into hours of delving into and

dialoguing in the word. Why wouldn't I honor such a man?

12) True spiritual fathers recommend their sons to and before other people. They speak well of their sons, approving them before other men. They ask other men to receive their sons as if they received them. The biblical account of Paul recommending Epaphroditus to the Philippian assembly is a great depiction of this (Philippians 2:25-30). My second spiritual father; Apostle Alex Mitala of Back to the Bible Truth (BBT) Mission in Nansana – Wakiso in Uganda is like Apostle Paul. This man of God knows the art of recommendation. He makes you feel accepted and received by other people. He prepared me for the United States of America. He spontaneously mentored and trained me in diplomacy, excellency, self-respect, time management and presentations before I met people in the USA and the rest of the world. He has mentioned my name, ability and skills before great people and he has also entrusted my brother and I to head a huge mentorship program called *Church Renewal* that will cover the entire continent of Africa. Such men are rare to find; and if you find one, honor him.

13) A relationship with a spiritual father is supernatural. There has to be a supernatural connection between spiritual fathers and sons. It is also organic, intentional and cannot be forced. One should not be coerced into it. It is sad when men of God coerce people into becoming their spiritual sons. Even though this relationship is supernatural, it is also my personal conviction that it is not possible to have a spiritual father you have never met, or will never meet physically. I think that, for a spiritual father to be effective, there has to be frequent and regular physical interaction. For those you have never met or will never meet, they are mentors, instructors and guardians (through their teaching materials), not spiritual fathers.

14) Control, manipulation, intimidation, surveillance, coercion, bullying, belittling, punishment, humiliation, fear, confusion, threats, pyramidal hierarchies and "heavy shepherding"[33] should never even

---

[33] Got Questions; What is Heavy Shepherding: Heavy shepherding" (also referred to as the "Discipleship Movement") is a method of psychological control used by abusive churches and cults. It came out

be whispered against a spiritual father. Spiritual fatherhood and son-ship is a life based on a warm relationship of freedom, liberty, free will, mutual honor and responsibility. Any "spiritual father" who exhibits any of the above negative traits should be avoided at all costs. They shouldn't be honored.

15) No one can be an effective spiritual father if they themselves failed at being sons to other spiritual fathers. If they grew up independently, were prideful, rejected and rebelled against spiritual leadership, how can they father others? How can they take others where they themselves have never been? How can they disciple people into spiritual disciplines they themselves have never been instructed in? Such men create an unhealthy environment of strife, intimidation, control, fear and manipulation; which environment does not facilitate healthy spiritual growth.

16) Spiritual fathers expand our thinking capacity. "A fathering presence helps enhance our grid of thinking and stretches us to see the big picture. It opens us up to more wisdom than decades of research and knowledge acquisition could provide," says Mark DeJesus in an article on the same subject in Charisma Magazine Online.[34]

17) A spiritual father offers spiritual leadership, prayer and intercession, prophetic declarations, sound wisdom and counsel, accountability, guidance, instruction and training. He rebukes, corrects and offers a sense of judgement. He encourages and comforts, offering discernment in cases of distractions, substitutions and deception.

He warns and protects against error and helps to focus his children in clarity of thought and purpose. He helps to interpret vision for those in this spiritual relationship with him.

of the Shepherding Movement of the 1970s. Retrieved from https://www.gotquestions.org/heavy-shepherding.html on 01/10/2018 at 4:12pm

[34]Mark DeJesus, Charisma Magazine (9/8/2016); Blessings You Can Receive From a True Spiritual Father, Retrieved from https://www.charismamag.com/life/relationships/27505-blessings-you-can-receive-from-a-true-spiritual-father on 9/28/2018 at 3:35am

18) Effective spiritual fathers are high-level strategic thinkers who have a global perspective of things. They encourage their sons to think about the world, not just about their surroundings or familiar environments. They stretch their sons to expand their vision, influence and also shoot them as arrows out of their quiver[35] to places they might never go. Apostle Charlie Ammons of RCC in Virginia, USA, is an example of a spiritual father who is a high-level strategic thinker with a global perspective, who also trains his sons to think globally and futuristically.

How Spiritual Sons Honor their Spiritual Fathers

"We are also enjoined to render honor as the best expression of good-will and gratitude toward them who best deserve in themselves, or most deserve of us; to our prince, to our parents, to our priests, especially to such of them as govern and teach well, to all good men." [36]

The relationship between a biological child and a great biological father can be compared to the relationship between a spiritual son (male and female) and a great spiritual father. When someone has a great biological father, the way they honor and relate to him is different from the way they will honor and relate to other people. So, if a man or woman, because of the relationship they have with their father (a relationship that you are not part of because that man is not your own father) is free to honor their own father the way they choose to, how do you judge the actions of those people in relation to their father? It would be very ridiculous for a wife of a certain man to get angry at another wife for the way she pampers her husband. The same natural principles apply to spiritual fathers and spiritual sons (male or female).

How, then, would a spiritual son (male and female) relate and honor a spiritual father that fits the criteria of a great biological father? Are there any limitations, rules, regulations, or set boundaries as to how far a son can go with their spiritual father? Scriptures have some examples we can look at.

---

[35]Psalm 127:3-5, New King James Version
[36]The Theological Works of Isaac Barrows, Volume I, Sermon VI: The Reward of Honoring God, Page 247

1) Gifts and presents: *Abraham and Melchizedek*
(Genesis 14; 18-20; Hebrews 7:1-10)

> *Hebrews 7:1-2: "This Melchizedek was king of Salem and priest of God Most High. He met Abraham returning from the defeat of the kings and blessed him, 2 and Abraham gave him a tenth of everything.... (NIV)."*

Abraham offered a tithe to Melchizedek because he recognized and perceived that this King of Salem was of a different order, and of a higher rank than him. He was a great priest of the Highest God, positioned above him to receive of his tithes. Even Levi, to whom tithes should be given, gave tithes to a higher Levite than him through the loins of Abraham. Sons can give gifts and presents to their spiritual fathers as an expression of honor. The same principle applies to meeting divine helpers. When you meet a great man, have a gift in your hand, it will make room for you before him. It is a way of honor.

2) Honor and obedience: *Moses and Jethro*
(Exodus 18:7, 24)

> *"So Moses went out to meet his father-in-law, bowed down, and kissed him. And they asked each other about their well-being, and they went into the tent. 24; So Moses heeded the voice of his father-in-law and did all that he had said (NKJV)."*

" Even Levi, to whom tithes should be given, gave tithes to a higher Levite than him through the loins of Abraham "

Jethro, a priest of Midian, was Moses' father-in-law. When he gave Moses counsel on how to judge the people, Moses took heed because he recognized him as his spiritual father. Besides physical expressions of honor, spiritual sons have to take heed to godly counsel and advice from their spiritual fathers.

48

3) Warriors, personal assistants, advocates, and intercessors: Joshua and Moses
(Exodus 17:13; 24:13; 33:11)

> *"So Joshua overcame the Amalekite army with the sword. Exodus 24:13; Then Moses set out with Joshua his aide, and Moses went up on the mountain of God. Exodus 33:11; The Lord would speak to Moses face to face, as a man speaks with his friend. Then Moses would return to the camp, but his young aide Joshua son of Nun did not leave the tent (NIV)."*

Spiritual sons fight their spiritual fathers' battles. Shocking truth! They advocate and represent them before opponents and accusers. Furthermore, they also wait on them as Personal Assistants (PA). In actual sense, a PA is the same as an armor bearer in the OT. It is rather weird, but true. Spiritual sons also pray, intercede and wait in the presence of the LORD for their spiritual fathers. 2 Timothy 4:11-13 prove that Timothy, Luke, John Mark and Tychicus were not only ministrial partners but also personal assistants to Paul.

4) Loyalty and pursuit: Ruth and Naomi
(Ruth 1:16-18)

> *"But Ruth replied, "Don't urge me to leave you or to turn back from you. Where you go I will go, and where you stay I will stay. Your people will be my people and your God my God. 17 Where you die I will die, and there I will be buried. May the Lord deal with me, be it ever so severely, if anything but death separates you and me." 18 When Naomi realized that Ruth was determined to go with her, she stopped urging her (NIV)."*

Spiritual sons (male and female) remain loyal to their spiritual fathers amidst adversity. They pursue these relationships with the resolve that death is the only reason for their ending. They forsake all others for the sake of their spiritual fathers. This is what Ruth did because of the honor she gave Naomi; no wonder she is one of the only two gentiles in the lineage of Jesus.

5) Service, integrity, faithfulness, true sonship: David and Saul
(1 Samuel 18:5; 24:5-7,11-12)

"So David went out wherever Saul sent him, and behaved wisely. And Saul set him over the men of war, and he was accepted in the sight of all the people and also in the sight of Saul's servants.

1 Sam 24:5-7: "Now it happened afterward that David's heart troubled him because he had cut Saul's robe. 6 And he said to his men, "The Lord forbid that I should do this thing to my master, the Lord's anointed, to stretch out my hand against him, seeing he is the anointed of the Lord." 7 So David restrained his servants with these words, and did not allow them to rise against Saul. And Saul got up from the cave and went on his way."
1 Sam 24:11-12: "Moreover, my father, see! Yes, see the corner of your robe in my hand! For in that I cut off the corner of your robe, and did not kill you, know and see that there is neither evil nor rebellion in my hand, and I have not sinned against you. Yet you hunt my life to take it. 12 Let the Lord judge between you and me, and let the Lord avenge me on you. But my hand shall not be against you (NKJV)."

David is the only man that the Bible calls, "a man after God's own heart". The above scriptures attest to this truth. David understood and walked in true honor even at the time when Saul did not deserve it. Spiritual sons serve their spiritual fathers without hesitation or reservation. A true spiritual son does not have a "but", "because", "if" or "maybe" when his spiritual father(s) seeks their help. Spiritual sons are willing, able and available to serve their spiritual father(s) at all times. True spiritual sons are so full of integrity that it hurts them to dishonor their spiritual fathers even in the slightest degree.

As long as their spiritual father(s) are still "reigning as sitting kings", spiritual sons will never do anything that undermines or is against the spiritual authority, position, or influence of their spiritual fathers. They will honor them. True spiritual sons will never "overthrow" their spiritual fathers in any way. They can never blackmail, or hurt the reputation and person of their spiritual fathers. Their hearts and the conscience of their souls are clear of all ill-motives and malicious intent towards their spiritual fathers. They will restrain those that submit to them not to speak ill of their spiritual fathers. In this regard, Apostle

Alex Mitala of BBT Mission in Nansana, Wakiso District, Uganda is a man above reproach. I have never heard him speak back to anyone who raises an accusation or verbal abuse against him. He does not even allow his sons to do the same to anyone who gets in a battle of words with him. He has always let the Lord avenge him. I want to emulate such men.

6) Covering of weakness and sins: Shem, Ham, Japheth and Noah (Genesis 9:20-23)

> "Noah, a farmer, was the first to plant a vineyard. 21 He drank from its wine, got drunk and passed out, naked in his tent. 22 Ham, the father of Canaan, saw that his father was naked and told his two brothers who were outside the tent. 23 Shem and Japheth took a cloak, held it between them from their shoulders, walked backwards and covered their father's nakedness, keeping their faces turned away so they did not see their father's exposed body." [37]

True spiritual sons will never expose or uncover the weaknesses, failures and sins of their spiritual fathers. Rather, they cover them with love and prayers, for love covers a multitude of sins (Proverbs 10:12). A son who maliciously and intentionally exposes, talks about, insinuates, hints, or opens up on their spiritual fathers' failures to a third party (anyone outside of their spiritual family) is not a true spiritual son and is not being honorable. The only allowance is for the issue to be dealt with within the family (Shem and Japheth got to know, but they did not see Noah's nakedness).

Having knowledge of your spiritual father's weaknesses is not evil, but releasing such information to third parties is what is evil. Shem and Japheth worked to protect their father's honor and not to damage it. This is what we ought to do. Whatever we do or say in such circumstances should be to protect our spiritual father's honor, not damage it. The same applies to other brethren in the faith who may not be at the level of our spiritual fathers. When you receive a negative or ridiculing forwarded post on your phone or email about them, do you also forward it or do you delete it? Why should you cause innocent souls

[37] THE MESSAGE: The Bible in Contemporary Language © 2002 by Eugene H. Peterson.

to have mixed feelings and sentiments about God's other children? The first story I mentioned at the beginning of this chapter where a man of God told me about his spiritual father's weaknesses damaged my weak conscious, so much so that I struggled for years to esteem and honor his spiritual father. If you can't do something to help your man of God in his failures, shut up! It is better to remain silent than to damage those who receive ministry from him.

7) Abandoning all else for that one Man of God: Elisha and Elijah (1 Kings 19:19,21)

> *"So Elijah went from there and found Elisha son of Shaphat. He was plowing with twelve yoke of oxen, and he himself was driving the twelfth pair. Elijah went up to him and threw his cloak around him. 21; So Elisha left him and went back. He took his yoke of oxen and slaughtered them. He burned the plowing equipment to cook the meat and gave it to the people, and they ate. Then he set out to follow Elijah and became his attendant (NIV)."*

After encountering his spiritual father, Elisha went back home and slaughtered his oxen, cooked the meat using the ploughing equipment and wood and fed his people. When he left his family to follow Elijah, he had no fall back plan. He recklessly abandoned everything to follow the man that he would later inherit a double portion of the anointing from. That is the same thing Jesus told the rich young ruler in Matthew 19:21-22, but because possessions were more important to him than following Jesus, he turned back sorrowful. Elisha honored Elijah and abandoned all for him, the rich young ruler honored his wealth more than he honored Jesus, no wonder he could not forsake all for Him.

True spiritual sons who are keen on being distinct in this world will abandon everything to follow a man God has anointed with the kind of anointing they desire. Through those men of God, spiritual sons see God in reality, the word becoming flesh, what is possible with God and how far they can go.

As spiritual sons follow a spiritual father who brings the reality of heaven to earth before their eyes, it will not matter how much negativity and criticism you will bring against their "man of God"; they will still honor and submit to him.

8) Running errands: Timothy and Paul
(2 Tim 4:9-13)

> *"Be diligent to come to me quickly; 10 for Demas has forsaken me, having loved this present world, and has departed for Thessalonica — Crescens for Galatia, Titus for Dalmatia. 11 Only Luke is with me. Get Mark and bring him with you, for he is useful to me for ministry. 12 And Tychicus I have sent to Ephesus. 13 Bring the cloak that I left with Carpus at Troas when you come — and the books, especially the parchments (NKJV)."*

The way a biological child can run errands for their biological father is the same way a spiritual son can run errands for their spiritual father. Spiritual fathers are free to ask their sons to do a few things for them because they trust that their sons will not think that they are being abused, used, or enslaved. True spiritual sons rejoice at the slightest opportunity of serving their spiritual fathers and receiving instructions from them. It won't feel burdensome. They serve out of honor, not duty.

9) Following the pattern and doctrine: Timothy and Paul
(2 Timothy 1:13,14; 1 Timothy 4:11, 6-7)

> *"Follow the pattern of the sound words that you have heard from me, in the faith and love that are in Christ Jesus. By the Holy Spirit who dwells within us, guard the good deposit entrusted to you."*

> *1 Timothy 4:11: "Command and teach these things (ESV)."*

> *1 Timothy 4:6-7: "If you put these things before the brothers, you will be a good servant of Christ Jesus, being trained in the words of the faith and of the good doctrine that you have followed. Have nothing to do with irreverent, silly myths. Rather train yourself for godliness (ESV)."*

A spiritual son who honors his spiritual father will follow his pattern of doing things, guard the deposit of the words entrusted to him by the man of God and encourage and teach others to do the same. A spiritual son who teaches against the teachings of his spiritual father is not a true spiritual son. A spiritual son will not depart from the doctrine, principles and way of life of his spiritual father. Being a good servant of Jesus Christ will depend on the way a spiritual son will follow the words of faith and of the good doctrine as taught by his spiritual father.

10) They finish their fathers' unfinished business: *Titus and Paul (Titus 1:4-5)*

> *"To Titus, my true son in our common faith: Grace and peace from God the Father and Christ Jesus our Savior. 5; The reason I left you in Crete was that you might straighten out what was left unfinished and appoint elders in every town, as I directed you (NIV)."*

True spiritual sons sort out their fathers' unfinished business, which is a true mark of honor. They clear their fathers' messes and straighten what got crooked. Spiritual sons also carry out new tasks that their parents were not able to do. They follow their spiritual fathers' directions to the dot, doing things the way they would want them done.

In doing this, the spiritual children remain loyal and honorable enough to implement their fathers' wishes. They don't seek attention. A true spiritual son who the Spirit of the Lord has blessed with deeper revelation and knowledge, will not preach against or attack what his spiritual father preached or taught. Rather, he will respectfully clarify any crooked doctrine and teaching. Subsequently, the spiritual son builds new walls of the gospel that his father was not able to set up. He builds on the foundation that his spiritual father laid.

11) Receiving other men on behalf of their spiritual fathers: Paul and the Philippian Church
(Philippians 2:25, 29)

> *"25 Yet I considered it necessary to send to you Epaphroditus, my brother, fellow worker, and fellow soldier, but your messenger and the one who ministered to my need; 29 Receive him therefore in the Lord with all gladness, and hold such men in esteem (NKJV)."*

54

The Philippians were Paul's spiritual sons. Whenever they needed help and discipleship, Paul often sent his ministry colleagues to them. On this occasion, Paul sent Epaphroditus, asking the Philippians to receive and esteem him on his behalf. He wanted them to honor Epaphroditus like they would have honored him.

True spiritual sons will receive and treat their spiritual father's recommended persons the same way they would have received and treated him; without reservation, hesitation, or minimal royalty. This is what Jesus meant when he said those who received those He sent were in actual sense receiving Jesus Himself (see Matthew 10:40).

How you receive your spiritual father's recommended person is a true reflection of how you value your spiritual father.

"Now, therefore, it was not you who sent me here, but God; and He has made me a father to Pharaoh and lord of all his household and ruler over all the land of Egypt." Joseph, Prime Minister of Egypt (Genesis 45:8, NKJV)

"Honor is a deep, deep abiding inner attitude of reverence and respect," Martin G. Collins

---

CHAPTER 5
LEADING THROUGH HONOR

"I WARN and counsel the elders among you (the pastors and spiritual guides of the church) as a fellow elder and as an eyewitness [called to testify] of the sufferings of Christ, as well as a sharer in the glory (the honor and splendor) that is to be revealed (disclosed, unfolded): 2 Tend (nurture, guard, guide, and fold) the flock of God that is [your responsibility], not by coercion or constraint, but willingly; not dishonorably motivated by the advantages and profits [belonging to the office], but eagerly and cheerfully; 3 Not domineering [as arrogant, dictatorial, and overbearing persons] over those in your charge, but being examples (patterns and models of Christian living) to the flock (the congregation). 4 And [then] when the Chief Shepherd is revealed, you will win the conqueror's crown of glory." [38]

"It is not titles that honor men, but men that honor titles." [39]

A few years ago, I heard of a story of a lady who attended a lunch-hour fellowship in the capital of a certain African country. It was alleged that at that time, her husband who was abroad, was sending her money to build their matrimonial home. At that fellowship, the weekly preachers would squeeze every last penny out of believers, with assurances of one hundredfold instant miraculous returns.

Through coercive preaching and spiritual manipulation, the woman "sowed" all the money expecting it to double in one week. It never did. She went back to the lunch hour fellowship asking them to refund

---

[38]Peter the Apostle, 1 Peter 5:1-4 Amplified Bible
[39]Niccolo Machiavelli, Brainy Quotes: Quotes on Honor. Retrieved from https://www.brainyquote.com/topics/honor, 27/09/2018, 5:09pm

the money, but they could not. Out of fear and panic, it was said that she committed suicide because she did not know how and what to tell her hardworking husband that she had lost the money in a lunch-hour fellowship.

The way we lead those that God has given us is proof to whether we honor or manipulate them.

Becoming worthy of Honor through Exceptional, Effective, and Responsible Leadership

Spiritual leadership is a gift of the grace of God. It is not obtained by merit. However, because we lead men and not God, it is our responsibility to honor the gift of God and the people that receive it, and be faithful stewards of the manifold grace of leadership. Even though leadership is a gift from God, execution of this gift in an exceptional way is costly. Understanding your responsibility as a spiritual leader will help you know and learn how to be a good steward of this gift and honor those you lead.

Exceptional and effective spiritual leaders should not sit on the sidelines of indecisiveness, lethargy, compromise, procrastination and mediocrity, but should be on the right side of diligence, compassion, integrity, commitment, purpose, excellence, exemplary behavior, honesty, faithfulness, hope, focus, passion, and humility. No wonder scriptures are not silent concerning leadership matters. Let us look at a few of them:

"The way we lead those that God has given us is proof to whether we honor or manipulate them"

1 Timothy 3:1-7: "1 The saying is true and irrefutable: If any man [eagerly] seeks the office of bishop (superintendent, overseer), he desires an excellent task (work). 2 Now a bishop (superintendent, overseer) must give no grounds for accusation but must be above reproach,

the husband of one wife, circumspect and temperate and self-controlled; [he must be] sensible and well behaved and dignified and lead an orderly (disciplined) life; [he must be] hospitable [showing love for and being a friend to the believers, especially strangers or foreigners, and be] a capable and qualified teacher, 3

"An exceptional spiritual leader must not have ground for any kind of accusation and reproach, whether in words or deeds"

Not given to wine, not combative but gentle and considerate, not quarrelsome but forbearing and peaceable, and not a lover of money [insatiable for wealth and ready to obtain it by questionable means]. 4 He must rule his own household well, keeping his children under control, with true dignity, commanding their respect in every way and keeping them respectful. 5 For if a man does not know how to rule his own household, how is he to take care of the church of God? 6 He must not be a new convert, or he may [develop a beclouded and stupid state of mind] as the result of pride [be blinded by conceit, and] fall into the condemnation that the devil [once] did. 7 Furthermore, he must have a good reputation and be well thought of by those outside [the church], lest he become involved in slander and incur reproach and fall into the devil's trap (AMP).

The books of Timothy and Titus have a very different tone compared to other Pauline epistles because in these two epistles, Paul writes to leaders and not to the flock. He sounds strict, instructive, corrective, and appears to warn these leaders. 1Timothy 3:1 says if any man desires a leadership position, he actually desires a good thing. However, in the same portion of scripture, Paul lists the cost of being an exceptional leader. Some people might not want to hear these kinds of instructions because they appear as legal rules and regulations to them. Such people forget that in the same book, Paul refers to a soldier[40]

[40]2 Timothy 2:3-6

of Christ as one who is not entangled in the affairs of this world. The life of a soldier is a life of total obedience to orders of higher ranks. No questions or requests for explanations are entertained; it is only obedience that is required. Military life is different from civilian life, and that is how leadership is. No wonder Strategic Leadership and Strategic Management developed from within the US military because of the kind of instructive training those people receive.

Paul also talks about the athlete who runs according to the rules, and also mentions the hardworking farmer. All these types of people he compares and refers Timothy to are very diligent and highly trained. They attribute their success to following instructions to the dot. Therefore, an exceptional spiritual leader must not have ground for any kind of accusation and reproach, whether in words or deeds.

There should be nothing to accuse or reproach a spiritual leader for. His name must not be dragged in any kind of disgraceful accusations and reproaches. A spiritual leader is a steward of God's gift. Therefore, as Paul writes in Titus 1:7, a spiritual leader must be blameless. This is the same point he stresses in 1Timothy 3. He ought to be honorable even among outsiders.

Fidelity and commitment to one wife should be binding factors of a leader's marriage. Sexual abstinence and chastity are mandatory for the unmarried spiritual leader. An honorable leader must reign over his household (which can also represent his physical body). He must keep his children under subjection and his house in order. The point is, if he cannot lead his house, how then can he lead and take care of the house of God?

An exceptional leader must be circumspect, temperate and self-controlled, because if he cannot rule his spirit,[41] how can he "rule" the spirits of other men? If a spiritual leader expects people to honor him, then he should also exhibit circumspection, temperance, and self-control. Sensibility, dignified behavior, disciplined and orderly lives, are what will distinguish an exceptional leader from the rest of the pack. He

[41] King Solomon, Proverbs 16:32, New King James Version

60

must be sensitive to the needs, strength, abilities, skills and weaknesses of those he leads.

> **"A leader's wife determines the hospitable atmosphere of a home or the lack of it"**

An exceptional leader must be hospitable, opening up his house to strangers. Hospitality has a blessing of entertaining angels[42] tied to it. However, a leader's wife determines the hospitable atmosphere of a home or the lack of it. If a man's wife does not welcome visitors and strangers, it does not matter how much her husband loves hospitality. Pastor Vikki Ammons, the wife of Apostle Charlie Ammons of RCC in Virginia – USA, and Mrs. Catherine Mitala, wife to Apostle Alex Mitala of BBT Mission Uganda are women of worth and excellence. They are hospitable, neat and organized. They are worth honoring. These are women whose sense of organization, hospitality and neatness are commendable.

Having a spiritual gift of leadership without leadership skills is like using a blunt axe to cut down a tree. The wise King Solomon writes and says, *"If the axe is dull and its edge unsharpened, more strength is needed, but skill will bring success."* [43] Developing leadership skills makes one a capable, skilled and qualified leader and teacher of the Word. Reading leadership materials from writers like Dr. John C. Maxwell is a starting point to raising your leadership lid. Joining Harvest Institute in Kampala, Uganda, a leadership training school started and run by Worship Harvest Ministries was one of the best decisions I ever made in my journey as a leader.

I am growing and improving in my leadership skills because of this school, and this book is a by-product of my enrolment to it. Leading with honor requires leadership skills and expertise.

---

[42] Hebrews 13:2
[43] Ecclesiastes 10:10, New International Version

A spiritual leader must not be a drunkard. Titus 1:8 calls it sobriety. Drinking a little wine is not a sin (controversially true[44]) in itself, but getting drunk is. However, habitual use of "a little" wine can lead to alcoholism because of its high alcoholic content of almost 14%. It won't be honorable if a spiritual leader is influenced, addicted to, or is an abuser of alcohol and other substances. (Disclaimer: I don't drink wine because alcoholism is a tribal problem where I come from. By the grace of God I try keep away from anything that can turn into an addiction).

A violent and abusive person should not be a leader. Gentleness, self-control, consideration of others, forbearance, long suffering, forgiveness, generosity and peace should be some of the character traits of a leader; beginning with the way they treats people in their home to the assembly of believers. Before a spiritual leader honors God, they should first honor those that live and interact with them.

There is no excuse for a spiritual leader to be quarrelsome. Titus 1:7 elaborates on this point. In this letter, Paul says a leader should not be self-willed, or easily angered. A self-willed person always wants things their own way. They are hard-hearted and non-compromising. Furthermore, they are non-accommodative and adamant, to the detriment of their relationships. A person who easily snaps has a very long way to becoming an effective and exceptional spiritual leader. If they assume leadership with these traits, they will constantly fall out with people. On the other hand, a temperate person; as

> " Before a spiritual leader honors God, they should first honor those that live and interact with them "

---

[44] 1 Timothy 5:23

Titus 1:7 puts it, is the opposite of a self-willed person. They govern, guard, and have their souls (emotions, mind and will) renewed by the Word every day. This is one of the greatest victories to possess in life. This is what a spiritual leader should strive for, and it is honorable.

A spiritual leader must not be a lover of money (insatiable for wealth and ready to obtain it by questionable means). No wonder Paul worked with his hands to meet his own needs . Today, many spiritual leaders twist the word of God to get money out of unsuspecting Christians. This is sad and should not be so. Money is not the source of all evil, but the love of it is . This is what Paul is dealing with here. Financial literacy, faithfulness, integrity, accountability and management are crucial in a spiritual leader's life. Mismanagement, corruption, misuse, misappropriation, swindling, diversion of resources and financial impropriety dishonor the leader, the gospel, and the name of the Lord.

A novice is a new convert and appointing them into spiritual leadership is a challenge. Such an amateur's heart is prone to pride, thereby leading them in the same snare like the devil. I am all for engagement and participation of everyone in ministry activities, but with leading teams, I suggest that we choose men and women who have grown in the faith and have served longer in the ministry. They should prove themselves faithful and diligent.

In this way, they will lead those on their teams with honor. Scriptures instruct spiritual leaders to have a good reputation among non-believers so as to avoid blackmail, slander and reproach. These are Satan's traps to discredit the name of the Lord and the free course of the gospel. Secondly, non-believers do not understand grace and compassion. They are naturally more prone to revenge, mob justice and evil practices because they have another spirit. These truths are expressed in some scriptures below.

> *2 Corinthians 6:1, 3-4: "We then, as workers together with him, beseech you also that ye receive not the grace of God in vain. 3; Giving no offence in anything, that the ministry be not blamed: 4; But in all things approving ourselves as the ministers of God."*

1 Timothy 3:2, 7: "A bishop then must be blameless...7; Moreover, he must have a good report of them which are without; lest he fall into reproach and the snare of the devil. 4:12: "Let no one despise your youth, but be an example to the believers in word, in conduct, in love, in spirit, in faith, in purity. 16 Take heed to yourself and to the doctrine. Continue in them, for in doing this you will save both yourself and those who hear you (NKJV)."

Titus 1:9: "Holding fast the faithful word as he hath been taught, that he may be able by sound doctrine both to exhort and to convince the gainsayers."

Philippians 2:14-16:"Do all things without complaining and disputing, 15 that you may become blameless and harmless, children of God without fault in the midst of a crooked and perverse generation, among whom you shine as lights in the world, 16 holding fast the word of life, so that I may rejoice in the day of Christ that I have not run in vain or labored in vain (NKJV)."

2 Peter 2:1-3: "But there were also false prophets among the people, even as there will be false teachers among you, who will secretly bring in destructive heresies, even denying the Lord who bought them, and bring on themselves swift destruction. 2 And many will follow their destructive ways, because of whom the way of truth will be blasphemed (NKJV)."

Luke 17:1-2: Then He said to the disciples, "It is impossible that no offenses should come, but woe to him through whom they do come! 2 It would be better for him if a millstone were hung around his neck, and he were thrown into the sea, than that he should offend one of these little ones (NKJV)."

It is possible for immature leaders to receive the grace of God in vain and to offend people in one way or another, which might bring reproach to the ministry. In all our affairs, we ought to approve ourselves as blameless servants of God, having a good report of them that are without. Without which we cannot convince the naysayers that the gospel is transformational. This is more so if they do not see a difference between them and us. Disputes and competition; whether in the gospel or not, will result in scandals. The Spirit of God instructs us to avoid disputes, competition or complaints. Resolving issues in peace with other people is godly and will save us a lot of other problems that come with them. By doing that, our light will shine brighter and it will be hard for crooked men in this perverted world to find fault or blame with us. Our race and labor in Christ will not be in vain.

Healthy confrontation on the other hand is good, and helps us to resolve problems in human relationships. However, people do not enjoy being confronted due to their inner insecurities. Such people are not fully yielded to the light of the gospel of Christ. Leading through honor trains a leader to utilize biblical and godly solutions to managing conflicts, disputes and scandals.

False ministers of the gospel will always be among us. It does not matter how many campaigns we do to expose false prophets and teachers, scripture affirms that they have always been there, and will always be. They will also continue to grow worse and worse. Unfortunately, because of their presence "the way of truth is blasphemed", causing believers and non-believers to be offended, and in turn to dishonor the gospel. That is how grave their actions to the body of Christ are. They are a liability to the gospel. Woe unto those through whom offences come! A spiritual leader must be an example in word, conduct, love, spirit, faith, and in purity so as to shield himself and those he leads against reproach. He must take heed to study sound doctrine, thereby depicting what a privilege and how honorable it is to serve the Lord.

The need for Training and Mentoring

Even if, as a spiritual leader, you never get an opportunity to go to seminary (most charismatic leaders despise going to bible school, arguing that theological schools quench and "dry" the Spirit and anointing on their lives) there is no excuse for lack of knowledge and ignorance in the gospel. Paul was one of the most gifted, charismatic, effective and exceptional leaders of all time, yet he valued training, study, education and mentorship. No wonder he wrote three quarters of the New Testament books of Holy Scriptures.

We can learn a whole lot from him as thus.

2 Timothy 2:15: "Study and be eager and do your utmost to present yourself to God approved (tested by trial), a workman who has no cause to be ashamed, correctly analyzing and accurately dividing [rightly handling and skillfully teaching] the Word of Truth (AMP)."

2 Timothy 4:13: "Bring the cloak that I left with Carpus at Troas when you come — and the books, especially the parchments (NKJV)."

Acts 5:34: "Then one in the council stood up, a Pharisee named Gamaliel, a teacher of the law held in respect by all the people, and commanded them to put the apostles outside for a little while." Acts 22:3: "I am indeed a Jew, born in Tarsus of Cilicia, but brought up in this city at the feet of Gamaliel, taught according to the strictness of our fathers' law, and was zealous toward God as you all are today (NKJV)."

An effective and exceptional spiritual leader is one who never tires from the discipline of learning and study. Anyone can be called of God, but few are approved as diligent workmen. Ignorance and lack of knowledge cause shame, embarrassment and dishonor, but correctly analyzing, accurately dividing, rightly and skillfully handling the Word of truth is profitable to both the minister and those he ministers to. On the discipline of study, J. Oswald Sanders writes, "The leader who intends to grow spiritually and intellectually will be reading constantly."[45] There can be no end to education.

Unfortunately, a survey conducted by the Jenkins Group in the US reported that, "42% of college graduates never read another book after

> **"An effective and exceptional spiritual leader is one who never tires from the discipline of learning and study..."**

[45] Sanders, J. Oswald. Spiritual Leadership/Spiritual Discipleship/Spiritual Maturity Set (Kindle Locations 2219-2220). Moody Publishers. Kindle Edition.

college."[46] After graduating from organized institutions of learning, many people never read any other book in their lives. They maintain that they read enough during school. Such a mind will never grow past its area of study, and without intentionality, there can never be new improvements in other areas of their lives.

"...Anyone can be called of God, but few are approved as diligent workmen"

The same can be applied to men and women on the pulpit. Without intentional personal study, research, reading and sitting under a mentor, a spiritual leader might never be effective and exceptional. Books give a spiritual leader access to and an audience with mighty men. "The leader should read to have fellowship with great minds. Through books we hold communion with the greatest spiritual leaders of the ages,"[47] writes J. Oswald Sanders.

Concerning 2 Timothy 4:13, Sanders writes, "Paul's books — the ones he wanted Timothy to bring along — were probably works of Jewish history, explanations of the law and prophets, and perhaps some of the heathen poets Paul quoted in his sermons and lectures. A student to the end, Paul wanted to spend time in study."[48] Taught under Gamaliel, a great teacher of the law, Paul's life was defined by training, mentorship, education, and study; to the extent that even after he converted from Judaism to Christianity, he kept this discipline.

With the availability of the internet, e-libraries, and great tools like Kindle, is there any excuse for a spiritual leader to be a mediocre when it comes to spiritual knowledge and revelation? It would be very unfortunate if they are. We honor those we lead if we are sound in doctrine and are able to teach.

---

[46] Skeptics Stack Exchange; www.skeptics.stackexchange.com, Retrieved on 03/10/2018 at 4:28pm
[47] Sanders, J. Oswald. Spiritual Leadership/Spiritual Discipleship/Spiritual Maturity Set (Kindle Locations 2259-2260). Moody Publishers. Kindle Edition
[48] ibid

Do we Honor God's flock?

The way we lead those that God has given us is proof of whether we honor or manipulate them. Ezekiel 34, 1 Peter 5:1-4 and Hebrews 13:17 are sobering portions of scriptures for spiritual leaders. The way we take care of God's people determines their spiritual health. Ezekiel prophesied concerning shepherds who eat the fat, cloth themselves with the wool, kill the fatlings and yet not feed the sheep.

He speaks of the diseased and the weak that have not been strengthened, the sick that have not been healed, the hurting and crippled that have not been bandaged, the stray that have not been brought back, the lost that have not been found; yet those that stayed have instead been ruled with hardheartedness and harshness. Those who strayed and those who got lost and fell into the hands of beasts and wolves became prey, were ravaged and hurt the more.

It is unfortunate what freedom of worship and separation of church and state have done. Anyone with a "revelation" can open up a church or start a denomination. Independence and lack of accountability have also made the situation worse.

Desperate Christians have been taken advantage of in a number of ways; from global denominations whose priests molest young boys and the cases concealed, to non-denominational pastors and prophets who split families; they perform fake miracles, sleep with other men's wives, molest young teenage girls, recruit young boys into same-sex relationships and do many more abominable things. There are countless stories of abuses against parishioners that have gone unresolved.

> **"The way we lead those that God has given us is proof of whether we honor or manipulate them**

In a number of countries around the world, desperate believers have been made to eat grass, drink urine, sprayed with insecticides, eaten soil, drank anointing oil or holy water, bought anointed hankies and blankets, and others burnt to ashes with the promise that they are going to heaven.

In the West, I have heard of a cult made up of wealthy men who molest girls as young as 13. They marry multiple wives by indoctrinating them with rewards in the afterlife. The Chief Shepherd admonishes us to nurture, guard, and guide the flock of God. The flock is not ours, we are just stewards with a divine responsibility.

The responsibility, amazingly, has perks that come with it, but the Chief Shepherd instructs us that that should not be the underlying motivation to take on the shepherding role on His behalf. And because He is a gentle Shepherd unlike us, He does not coerce or constrain us from leading the flock. He asks us to willingly, eagerly and cheerfully lead.

The Chief Shepherd does not expect us to dominate, dictate, or arrogantly load it over those in our charge, but to be examples, patterns, and models of Christian living.

When the flock looks at us, they should not tell the difference between us and the Chief Shepherd. That is how identical to Him we should be. When we do this, we are leading honorably. Why does the Chief Shepherd give us all those instructions? Because one day we shall stand before Him to give an account of every sheep that He put under our care. Scary, right? It shouldn't be.

Some people have been so hurt by the "church" that they are not willing to return, unless God Himself brings them back.

"As I live, says the LORD God, surely because My sheep became a prey, and My sheep became food for every beast of the field because there was no shepherd — neither did My shepherds search for My sheep, but the shepherds fed themselves and fed not My sheep — 9 Therefore, O you [spiritual] shepherds, hear the word of the Lord: 10 Thus says the LORD God: Behold, I am against the shepherds, and I will require My sheep at their hand and cause them to cease feeding the sheep, neither shall the shepherds feed themselves any more. I will rescue My sheep from their mouths, that they may not be food for them. 11 For thus says the LORD God: Behold, I, I Myself, will search for My sheep and will seek them out."
(Ezekiel 34:8-11)

CHAPTER 6

HONORABLE DISCERNMENT

"Don't suppress the Spirit, 20 and don't stifle those who have a word from the Master. 21 On the other hand, don't be gullible. Check out everything, and keep only what's good. 22 Throw out anything tainted with evil." [49]

I once visited a local church in a village where I met Angelina. She was a beautiful dark-skinned, round-faced girl with big-eyes. Besides her beauty, she was a very gifted worship leader with a silky voice. However, like all of us, although her personality was different, her character was still under transformation by God's Spirit. One of the young women in the local church started a rumor "out-of-the-blue" that Angelina was a devil's agent! In those early years, such stories of devil's agents and Satan's letters (to local churches) were rampant in my country. The rumor spread like wild fire in that small village church!

About three other young women came up with allegations and accusations that Angelina mysteriously cut holes in their clothes as a

---

[49] 1 Thessalonians 5:19-22; THE MESSAGE: The Bible in Contemporary Language © 2002 by Eugene H. Peterson. All rights reserved.

witchcraft attack (they used to share clothes). Almost all the young people (including males) in that local village church believed the rumor. Angelina was the black sheep in an all-white flock! She was segregated against, maligned, criticized, and talked about by fellow brethren. Her world was falling apart. It was not after the coming of a music minister from another church that had come to train this local church's worship team that Angelina was part of that the rumor was crashed by the music minister's apostolic gift. What Angelina suffered was a false "discernment" from her fellow young people from their local church.

- -

Discernment is very crucial in the practice of Honor. That is why I have written an entire chapter to try and expound its intricacies. Lack of discernment has led many believers to false ministers of the gospel, and at the same time its misunderstanding has left many innocent believers and ministers labeled as false yet they are not. Understanding and growing in true discernment will help us to know how and who to honor.

Discernment is one of the most complicated spiritual gifts. The body of Christ generally looks into discernment only when trying to figure out evil spirits and false prophets.[50] Even though discernment has a component of that, it means a lot more. Most folks in the Kingdom of God mistake other workings of the soul as discernment, yet they are not. We shall first demystify what discernment is not.

> **"Understanding and growing in true discernment will help us to know how and who to honor"**

What it is Not

The *Macmillan English Dictionary*[51] will guide us in understanding some of these words as we try to explain what discernment is not.

---

[50] 1 Corinthians 12:10; 1 John 4:1
[51] Macmillan English Dictionary for Advanced Learners CD-ROM 2nd Edition. CD-ROM © Macmillan Publishers Limited 2007. Text © A&C Black Publishers Ltd 2007.

Skepticism: This is, "doubt that someone has about something that other people think is true or right." To the natural mind, this sounds like discernment. However, since the Spirit of God does not give us doubt, being doubtful means that you have not discerned right.

Criticism: "comments that show that you think something is wrong or bad." Thinking that something is wrong or bad does not make it so. It might just be your opinion that springs out of your fear for the uncommon occurrences of the Spirit and the supernatural.

Suspicion: "A feeling that someone has done something wrong." What if your feelings change? Because they do. Will you still feel the same way for that minister of God? The Christian life is not based on feelings, but on faith. Personal feelings don't guarantee that what you feel is truth. Suspicion breeds gossip, from gossip it graduates to slander. All these are not the fruit of the Spirit; they are something else.

Cynicism: "The belief that things will not be successful or useful." The moment you think that a fellow Christian will not succeed, it is the first indicator that you are not discerning correctly. It could be that you wish them bad.

Contempt: "A feeling that someone or something is unimportant and deserves no respect." This is very true with those who are quick at "discerning" prophetic people as false prophets. If someone has no regard for prophetic gifts and supernatural ministry, their normal attitude towards them will always be contempt, which they will unconsciously interpret as discernment.

Prejudice: "Preconceived opinion that is not based on reason or actual experience." Many of us cannot discern because we have already set our minds to believing or seeing things a certain way, even without having a personal experience of them. Preconceived opinions do not measure up to actual experiences. A certain man of God said, "A man with an experience is not at the mercy of the man with an argument." Discernment is not based on prejudices, sentiments and arguments, but on personal and physical experiences from, with, and through God as we relate with other people.

Fear: "To feel afraid of someone or something because they might harm you." God has not given us the spirit of fear, but of love, power and a sound mind.[52] This fear might be springing from past encounters or it might spring right from the pits of hell to keep you away from encountering the presence of the Almighty God demonstrated through a human vessel.

The presence of fear in your heart is the absence of love, yet God is love.[53] A sound mind is one that has been renewed, transformed and tuned to the mind of Christ.

Hate: "To dislike someone or something very much." God is love and in Him there is no hate. Whoever does not love does not know God.[54] Disliking someone is a sign that you do not have God's kind of love for that person, and if you don't, then there is no way you can have the right discernment. Hate and love cannot abide together.

Bias: "Preferring one person, thing, or idea to another in a way that is unfair." Some Christians are biased against certain ministerial gifts, especially against prophetic people. They think prophetic people are weird (and sometimes they are), but preferring a certain gift over another is not right either. It is being carnal.[55] God supplied every gift for our spiritual good. If you are biased, you cannot discern rightly. Period.

Unbelief (unbelievable): "Too unlikely to be true or believed." Not being certain about something does not mean that it is not true. If something is too unlikely to be true, it could also mean that it is true. Having either doubt or unbelief for a certain gift in manifestation is sure evidence that you do not have true discernment. God must deal with your doubt and unbelief first before you can discern.

---

[52] 2 Timothy 1:7
[53] 1 John 4:8, 16
[54] ibid
[55] 1 Corinthians 3:1-8, New King James Version

74

Assumption: "Something that you consider likely to be true even when no one has told you directly or even when you have no proof." Isn't this how many innocent desperate souls have been led into deception just because there is some kind of manifestation? Evidence of supernatural manifestations is not a guarantee that their source is God. Assuming that God has sent someone does not mean that person is from God. They might just be a wolf in sheep's skin.[56]

Misinformation: "False or incorrect information…." If you do not have ALL the information concerning a servant of God, you must not make prejudiced judgment. Some of this information could be their background story of salvation, where they started from in the ministry, their contacts and their friends. You must also consider their theology and beliefs. Look up the number of sermons they have preached or books they have written. You will understand their thought pattern and inherent core beliefs from all these sources. It would be very hard for you to correctly discern someone without all this background knowledge. Rumors and hearsay do not accrue to discernment.

Misinterpretation and misjudgment: Misinterpretation: "A wrong way of understanding or explaining something." Misjudgment: "To make a wrong judgment about a person or situation." Without all the facts (misinformation), misinterpretation and misjudgment are inevitable. True discernment is way different from these.

Accusation: "A claim that someone has done something illegal or wrong." Misinformation, misinterpretation and misjudgment lead to false accusations. When we accuse people, we are not being honorable towards them. Accusation and discernment do not walk hand in hand. One is from "the accuser of the brethren"[57] and the other is from the Spirit of Grace. An accusatory spirit cannot discern at the same time and a spirit that cannot discern cannot honor.

Not always about demons: Limiting discernment to only the 'testing of spirits' waters down its significance. 1 Thessalonians 5:21

---

[56]Matthew 7:15, New King James Version
[57]Zechariah 3:1-2; Revelation 12:10

admonishes us to "test" everything, not just spirits or prophecy, but everything in life. Test everything that concerns you, not just evil spirits attacking you or lurking in the air. If searching for the presence of demons is the only thing a person does, there is a problem. This default setting will hinder and obstruct them from seeing past demonic presence.

Demon-consciousness actually attracts more demons in one's discernment function and life. Contrary to what most people do, we should not throw away everything deemed evil after "discerning" it. God wants us to "hold on to what is good". In other words, after you have tested all things, see the good; choose it out, focus and build on that! Disregard the evil. After this, you can leave and throw out any form of evil. A person whose *sole focus* is to abstain from any form of evil has not learnt to discern well.

Matthew 16:1-4 reveals another important aspect of discernment called "discerning the times". Knowledge of your season, times and signs sets you above what demons can do to hinder you. 1 John 4:1-4[58] cautions us not to believe everything we hear, but to carefully weigh and examine what people say and listen to their spirits, because by listening beyond their physical words about God lies a subtle lying spirit of error and deception. They will be preaching Jesus Christ, yet when you listen beyond their physical words and listen to their spirits by discernment, you can know that they operate under the spirit of evil. The only reason a child of God can listen beyond physical words is because greater is He that is in them than the spirit of error and deception that is in deceitful preachers who have been loosed in the world.

What Discernment is

Now that we have set the foundation by looking at what discernment is not, we shall progress and look at what it is. Discern comes from a Greek root word called *diakrino* **(dee-ak-ree'-no)**; which means "to separate thoroughly"[59]. Discernment is a gift of the Spirit, so it

---

[58]THE MESSAGE: The Bible in Contemporary Language © 2002 by Eugene H. Peterson. All rights reserved.
[59]Biblesoft's New Exhaustive Strong's Numbers and Concordance with Expanded Greek-Hebrew Dictionary. Copyright © 1994, 2003, 2006 Biblesoft, Inc. and International Bible Translators, Inc.

is not the result of the human soul (mind, will and emotions). We experience it through God's Spirit. With that in mind, we can now define discernment as *"Seeing, distinguishing, scrutinizing and separating spiritual truth, entities, activity and spiritual states thoroughly through the channel of the regenerated spirit"*, as explained below;

1) **Seeing/perception:** Spiritual eyes[60] that see what lies beyond the physical realm.

2) **Distinguishing/separating:**[61] Learning to spiritually sieve good from evil.

3) **Scrutinizing:** Spiritual analysis of spiritual sources.[62]

4) **Spiritual truth:** Going beyond what people say to the source of their ministration. Is it the Spirit of Truth or the cunning spirit of deception? (1 John 4:1-3).

5) **Spiritual entities:** All kinds of spirits and entities in the spiritual realm, whether good or evil.[63]

---

[60] The story that Jesus tells of the rich man and Lazarus in Luke 16:19-25 is an eye opener to the likeness of the human spirit. It is a story of spirits in the afterlife, yet these spirits "lift up their eyes and see", they also "feel the torment of the flames", they also "remember their relatives on earth", and also "feel the comfort in Abraham's boson". This story proves that the spirit of man has a spiritual function that supplies it with sight, taste, hearing, feeling, touch, and sense. Even though psychologists hijacked this organ and attributed it to the soul, conscience is a spiritual function that is way different from conscious which is of the soul.

[61] Hebrews 5:14; the senses talked about in this verse are not physical but spiritual as explained above. The Greek word used literally means "an organ of perception", but perception is not of the physical eyes but of the spiritual. Jesus discerned a lot by perception/perceiving.

[62] Acts 16:16-18 has the story of the slave girl who had a spirit of divination. The "words of knowledge" she proclaimed on Paul and Silas were actually accurate, but their source was the cunning one. If Paul depended on the accuracy of the girl's words and not looked at their source, they would have been deceived like so many of us are today. It is not about accuracy, it is the source that matters. The spirit of divination is very cunning and accurate in delivery, and can even confess the name of God, yet evil in nature, right from the kingdom of darkness.

[63] 1 Corinthians 15:32; Theologians debate at what Paul meant by "fighting beasts" at Ephesus, but whether literal or allegorical, I wish to submit that these beasts ruled the city before the gospel invaded it. Is it coincidental that in Chapter 1 and 6 of Ephesians Paul names a hierarchy of spiritual entities? Ephesians 6:12; 1:21, and Colossians 1:16 gives us this list; principalities, powers, rulers of darkness, spiritual hosts of wickedness, thrones, dominions, might, and names. Acts 19:24-35 proves that the city of Ephesus belonged to the goddess "Diana". What if behind the idol of Diana was a real spiritual beast that Paul fought with?

6) **Spiritual activity:** What goes on in the spiritual realm for or against the child of God and the gospel.[64]

7) **Spiritual states:** The spiritual condition, circumstance, environment and atmosphere in a given place, space or time.[65]

What True Discernment involves

True discernment is a gift and work of the Spirit of God in the spirit of man. Like all spiritual gifts whose mastery comes by exercise, one must exercise their spirits to grow and progress in discernment. The beginning point is to know what discernment involves. I shall try to expound on this as follows:

- **Discernment by the Word – (Proverbs 2:1-13):** When a person opens their spirit up and allows the word of God to enter and settle in, they sharpen their ability to discern. If they continue to seek spiritual wisdom, insight, knowledge, the fear of the LORD and understanding, the word shades light[66] to their spirit and they begin to discern by the word of God. This is possible because the light of the word of God exposes bare[67] all things that are contrary to sound doctrine.[68]

This is the foundation of true discernment where all other components fall. True discernment leads to honorable kingdom living because in exercising true discernment lies the art of truly treating people right. If you discern them right, you will treat them right. If you discern them wrong, you will treat them wrong.

- **Spiritual Understanding – (1 Kings 3:9-12; Job 12:12-13):** Spiritual understanding gives a person the ability to govern, discern right and wrong, administer justice and walk in divine wisdom. The more someone matures in spiritual understanding, the more they will advance in discernment. By and by, they will be more aware of

---

[64] Daniel 10:12-14, Luke 10:18 and 1 Thessalonians 2:18 give us a snapshot of activities in the spiritual realm for or against the child of God and the gospel

[65] Acts 17:16; Now while Paul waited for them at Athens, his spirit was provoked within him when he saw that the city was given over to idols. (NKJV)

[66] Psalm 119:130

[67] Hebrews 4:12

[68] Titus 1:9; 2:1; 1 Timothy 1:9-10; 2 Timothy 4:3

their spiritual surrounding as they press on into the things of the Spirit.

- **Spiritual Knowledge – (1 John 2:20):** The Greek word for "know" used in this verse literally means "to SEE"[69]. Spiritual knowledge then, involves seeing by the Spirit. It is a kind of inner knowledge that cannot be taught in a classroom. It is taught by the Spirit of God.

- **Spiritual Witness – (Romans 8:16):** As we exercise our spirits, the Spirit of God bears witness with our spirit about certain things. In experience, it "feels" as if there are two entities inside of you. It "feels" as if someone is beckoning your spirit to "see" something. There should be no conflict between the human spirit and the Spirit of God. After the human spirit has "agreed" with the Spirit of God, then discernment happens.

- **Spiritual Instruction – (John 16:13, 1 John 2:27):** Jesus told His disciples that when the Spirit of Truth comes He would guide them into all truth. This is the anointing that teaches Jesus' disciples all things. It is likened to a tour guide or a classroom instructor that you must follow along the path of truth.

- **Spiritual Senses – (Hebrews 5:14):** These spiritual senses are exercised through conscience; an organ of the spirit. They involve conviction, perception, impression, conception, prompting, intuition, communion and fellowship in the regenerated spirit of man. These senses also include; acknowledgment (epignosis), inference, groaning, agitation, indignation, a "moving" in your spirit (one of the rarest), urgency, nudge and burden. Expounding on each of these senses will be outside the bounds of our discussion so I shall leave it that.

- **Collusion of spirits – (Acts 16:16-18):** The story of Paul and the slave girl who had a spirit of divination is talked about in footnote 87. I expound on it here by saying that; in the spiritual realm, the spirit of Paul collided with the spirit of divination in the slave girl. He was agitated. The spirit of divination tried to appease Paul by giving him accurate "words of knowledge", which he didn't fall for. Have you ever met a person that the moment they set their eyes

---

[69] **eido (i'-do):** Biblesoft's New Exhaustive Strong's Numbers and Concordance with Expanded Greek-Hebrew Dictionary. Copyright © 1994, 2003, 2006 Biblesoft, Inc. and International Bible Translators, Inc.

on you they hate or become furious with you from the very start? It is because they are operating under the spirit of divination and sorcery. There was a collision of spirits in the spiritual realm; one of light, and another of darkness.

- **Spiritual experiences – (dreams, visions, trances and raptures):** We need to be cautious with spiritual experiences in this category because, not every dream, vision or trance is from the Spirit of truth. Many have been misled by *heavily* relying on them. Test every spiritual experience with the Word of God. Some of these experiences come from the soul; which is open to demonic interference. It can only be kept secure by renewing the mind. Let us endeavor to exercise the mind of Christ and set our affections on things above.

- **Discernment by Love – (Philippians 1:9-10):** Sincere love abounds more and more in full discernment of knowledge and perception by examining excellent things. With this kind of love, there is no place for offences, because offenses hinder the expression of love and lead to dishonorable lifestyles. Loving without offense will train one to discern as Christ discerns. Love keeps no record of wrongs. It separates what people do from who they are. Love covers a multitude of sins; therefore, love can discern without being judgmental, accusatory or envious. Love is the highest progression and level in discernment

Why we Fail to Discern

1. **Ignorance, lack of knowledge and gullibility – (Proverbs 1:22; 14:15; Hosea 4:6; 2 Timothy 4:3):** The ignorant or the simple are those that are gullible. They are easily seduced and reject or can't stand sound doctrine. They believe every word without discerning any of it. Lack of knowledge is caused by limited access to knowledge. Without spiritual knowledge, spiritual understanding and spiritual wisdom; there cannot be discernment.

2. **Carnality, sensuality and biases – (1 Corinthians 3:1-3, James 3:15, Jude 19, Romans 8:7):** Anyone who walks under the control and leadership of their carnal senses cannot at the

same time walk in discernment because discernment is not of the soul. A carnal person will take sides between ministers of God, biased for or against the other. They use earthly wisdom to cause or be part of confusion and divisions. Earthly wisdom evidenced in carnality, sensuality and biases is demonic and gives no place to the Spirit of God.

3. **The lust of the eyes and itching ears – (1 John 2:16, 2 Timothy 4:3):** Lustful eyes have a strong selfish desire and longing to be appeased by supernatural forces. On the other hand, itching ears want to hear what they selfishly want, rejecting anything outside appeasement and amusement. Any person in that category cannot discern the things of the Spirit.

4. **Deception – (1 Timothy 4:1, 2 Corinthians 11:3):** The very first snare of the cunning one from the very beginning has been deception. He has mastered the art of deception out of many centuries of practice and use. It is the same tactic he uses to take the innocent captive. A person who has fallen for the devil's deception and craftiness painted as truth fails to discern how blind they are or how deceptive the devil can be.

5. **Evil consciousness and preoccupation – (1 Timothy 4:2, Titus 1:15, Hebrews 10:22):** Scriptures admonish us, over and over again, to have a pure conscience toward all things and God. The state of our conscience determines our perception of different things. An evil conscience perceives evil and a pure conscience perceives pure things. However, when one's conscience has been seared with hot iron, it gets corrupted and they cannot walk in pure discernment. People who are preoccupied with demons attract more demonic activity. In the process, as their conscience continues to be fixed on that, they falsely discern the demonic even where there are no demons.

6. **Overly focused on miracles, signs and wonders – (Matthew 16:1-4; 12:28, John 6:30):** An evil and perverse generation *only* seeks after miracles, signs and wonders. They only want to believe after they have seen. They have selfish desires and put God on a pedestal, demanding a sign from Him so that they can believe. It is as if He is indebted to them. Those who *only* seek

after signs are deceived and blind. When they find one ready to perform for a show to prove their credibility, they fail to discern that he/she is not from God. Miracles, signs and wonders do not prove God's power and presence. God approves miracles, signs and wonders. His Word is independent and perfect with or without miracles, signs and wonders because even Satan can perform them.

Discerning a false minister

I shall not focus so much on what shows that a man or woman is false, because usually, a true and false minister are identical in so many ways. Remember that from a distance, wheat and tares look exactly the same. Therefore, it would be difficult to discern by looking for physical signs or certain words and phrases. However, these three things below can easily help you to discern a false minister of the Gospel.

i) **Multiple sexual relationships – (2 Peter 2:12-16):** This is very different from a person having a weakness for the opposite sex. It extends to ritual sex because it is a spiritual exchange of covenants with demons. The kingdom of darkness uses sex as a mode of communication and transferance of evil spirits and powers. Show me a false prophet and I shall show you a man(or woman) who entices unstable souls and indulges them in multiple sexual relationships, orgies and pervasions.

ii) **From revelation to methods – (Matthew 9:27-30; 12:22, Mark 10:46-52, John 9:6-7):** Jesus sets a precedent on how the supernatural happens. From observing His life and ministry, we learn that the supernatural life manifests spontaneously. There is no strict script to follow. Take an example of when He opened blind eyes; in Matthew 9:23 he touched the blind man and healed him. In Matthew 12:22, the scripture does not record Jesus doing anything, but he healed the blind man. Mark 10:46 talks of blind Bartimaeus whom Jesus healed by just speaking a word. In John 9:6-7 we find a man born blind who got healed when Jesus spat on the ground, mixed dirt with his saliva and put it on his eyes. Jesus then commanded the man to go and wash in a pool. In all these instances, Jesus NEVER repeated a "method", but healed each man differently because He didn't want us to rely on methods. Jesus wants us to rely on the free Spirit who works as He wills, spontaneously! When one makes a one-time revelation of a miracle a method and formula, they error and are susceptible to deception.

iii) The kind of spirit they have – (Luke 9:51-55, 2 Peter 3:9): In Luke, we find that once, Jesus was going to Jerusalem passing through Samaria. However, the Samaritans did not receive Him. His disciples (James and John) asked Him if He wanted them to command fire to come down from heaven and consume them, just as Elijah did. Jesus rebuked them saying; "You do not know what manner of spirit you are of. For the Son of Man did not come to destroy men's lives but to save them." There are instances that call for "holy anger" and zeal for God. However, these are different for a man whose "default setting" for their ministration and supernatural experiences are doom, destruction, calamity. If judgment, condemnation, accusation, revenge, anger, shame, hopelessness, negativity, evil consciousness and demonic pre-occupation are all a minister preaches, it is probable they are of "another spirit" that is not of God. That person may be accurate in what they do, but as long as there is doom-and-gloom in their thoughts, words and actions, it is likely that they operate under the spirit of divination and sorcery.

The Son of Man did not come to destroy men's lives, but to save them. He does not want anyone to perish, but that all should come to repentance. If someone thinks that God wants to destroy people's lives because they have sinned and are broken, they need to rethink their stance.

However sinful they are, no one has the right to call for their destruction by fire, accidents or different calamities. Such a minister does not operate under the Spirit of Grace and compassion that was demonstrated by Jesus Christ.

"For the word of God is living and active. Sharper than any double-edged sword, it penetrates even to dividing soul and spirit, joints and marrow; it judges the thoughts and attitudes of the heart. 13 Nothing in all creation is hidden from God's sight. Everything is uncovered and laid bare before the eyes of him to whom we must give account." (Hebrews 4:12-13)

CHAPTER 7

HONOR BIRTHS IMPARTATION

1 Sam 10:10-13: "10 When they came there to the hill, there was a group of prophets to meet him; then the Spirit of God came upon him, and he prophesied among them. 11 And it happened, when all who knew him formerly saw that he indeed prophesied among the prophets, that the people said to one another, "What is this that has come upon the son of Kish? Is Saul also among the prophets?" 12 Then a man from there answered and said, "But who is their father?" Therefore it became a proverb: "Is Saul also among the prophets?" 13 And when he had finished prophesying, he went to the high place." [70]

As people honor one another, a transaction happens in the spiritual realm that normally goes unnoticed because one cannot physically see what happens when it is taking place. This is what has theologically been termed as impartation. Understanding impartation is important in honor because of the following reasons:

1) So that people take advantage of the benefits of honor

2) So that people are careful as they choose the spiritual leaders they want to honor

3) To avoid receiving (spiritual) things they are not prepared or ready

---

[70] 1 Samuel 10:10-13, New King James Version

for because of the positive and negative effects involved in impartation.

Greek interpretation

'Impart' comes from a Greek word called *metadidomi (met-ad-id'-o-mee)*, which simply means "to give over, i.e. share." The root word for metadidomi is the Greek word *metathesis (met-ath'-es-is)*, which means "transposition, i.e. transferal (to heaven), disestablishment (of a law)." The very final root word for metathesis is the Greek word *metatithemi (met-at-ith'-ay-mee)*, which means, "to transfer, i.e. (literally) transport, (by implication) exchange (reflexively) change sides, or (figuratively) pervert.[71] Putting the above in consideration, impartation would then be defined as *"to give over, share, transpose, transfer, transport, transmit and exchange a spiritual deposit from one individual to another by supernatural means."* With this description in mind, impartation, therefore, takes a whole new significance in honor. To make my case, I shall submit a few scriptures that refer to this mystery either literally, or by inference:

> *2 Kings 2:9: "And so it was, when they had crossed over, that Elijah said to Elisha, "Ask! What may I do for you, before I am taken away from you?" Elisha said, "Please let a double portion of your spirit be upon me." (NKJV)*

> *2 Kings 2:15: "Now when the sons of the prophets who were from Jericho saw him, they said, "The spirit of Elijah rests on Elisha. And they came to meet him, and bowed to the ground before him." (NKJV)*

> *1 Corinthians 6:17: "But he who is joined to the Lord is one spirit with Him." (NKJV)*

Did Elijah transfer God's Spirit to Elisha or Elijah's own spirit? I think that what was imparted into Elisha was not only the anointing of God's Spirit, but also Elijah's kind of spirit in the process. When the sons of the prophets on the other side of the Jordan looked at Elisha after he had received a double portion of Elijah's spirit, they also affirmed and

[71] Biblesoft's New Exhaustive Strong's Numbers and Concordance with Expanded Greek-Hebrew Dictionary. Copyright © 1994, 2003, 2006 Biblesoft, Inc. and International Bible Translators, Inc.

confirmed that indeed the spirit of Elijah rested on Elisha. For the New Testament believer, born of the Spirit of God, I still think that this is applicable.

When we come to the Lord we become ONE spirit with Him. His Spirit is fused into our spirits and the two become one. From that point, there should be no difference in operation between the Spirit of Christ and our spirit. Remember that 1 Corinthians chapter 6 talks about sexual relationships and how they make two people become one. In that same chapter, the Spirit of God highlights a spiritual reality that is identical to what happens between two people becoming one flesh through sexual union. This should prove that spiritual fathers give of, share from, transfer, transport, transposition and exchange their kind of spirits with their spiritual sons.

> **Impartation is a complex phenomenon; that is why Elijah told Elisha that it was a difficult thing to ask (2 Kings 2:10). It only happens to those who honor those that God has set before them**

During my lifetime in the gospel, I have seen men who minister exactly like their spiritual fathers. Sometimes even their voices are identical to the voices of their fathers. Apart from a few exceptions, a miracle-worker normally raises miracle workers, a teacher raises teachers, a prophet raises prophets, an apostle will also produce apostles and so on and so forth. In practicing honor, you receive your spiritual father's kind of spirit. Elisha received of Elijah's spirit because he honored him. There can be no impartation without honor. Not only did he honor Elijah, but he served him in the meanest errands like "pouring water on the hands of Elijah (2 Kings 3:11)." So, before you desire to receive an impartation from any servant of God, make sure that honor is your lifestyle. What you desire from the one God has set before you determines how "much" honor you will give them. Elisha risked everything, and went the extra mile because of what he saw in Elijah. He did everything he could to receive of it.

Impartation is a complex phenomenon; that is why Elijah told Elisha that it was a difficult thing to ask (2 Kings 2:10). It only happens to those who honor those that God has set before them. If you take the anointing or call of God on someone else for granted, do not expect to receive of their spirit. The only condition that Elijah gave Elisha was if he would see him taken to heaven. This requirement for him to "see" was not just a physical requirement, but a spiritual one too. Elisha had to perceive the spiritual realm and the activities at that moment. This is perception. If we fail to perceive and acknowledge those that God has uniquely endowed with the anointing and gifts then we cannot receive an impartation from them. How we perceive others determines how they impact our lives.

> **A spiritual father has a supernatural ability to deposit a spiritual gift through impartation to his spiritual children. However, the spiritual children must also honor the parent to receive from them**

Paul writes to Timothy, his spiritual son, to stir up God's gift in him. However, for Timothy to receive this gift, his spiritual father Paul must prophesy and lay hands on him. Timothy needed the elders to deposit this gift into him before he could stir it up. A spiritual father has a supernatural ability to deposit a spiritual gift through impartation to his spiritual children. However, the spiritual children must also honor the parent to receive from them.

> *2 Timothy 1:6: "Therefore, I remind you to stir up the gift of God which is in you through the laying on of my hands." (NKJV)*

> *1 Timothy 4:14: "Do not neglect the gift that is in you, which was given to you by prophecy with the laying on of the hands of the eldership." (NKJV)*

> *In Romans 1:11 the scriptures say: "For I long to see you, that I may impart to you some spiritual gift, so that you may be established." (NKJV)*

Paul, having been received as an apostle and spiritual father to the Romans, longed to go over to them and give of, share from, transfer, transmit, transport, transposition and exchange some spiritual gifts to and with the Romans. It is as if he had them stored somewhere (of course in his spirit) that he could just pick out some and give to the Romans. Some will reject these possibilities, but I shall not fear to assert that regardless of whom a spiritual son opens up their spirits to, a spiritual father will pick out from his storage of spiritual gifts and distribute amongst his sons. We must remember, though, that this must be honorably done. We have access to God's supernatural storehouse of gifts. It is from here that He allows His servants to distribute them to His people. It is also notable that impartation establishes the receiver of the supernatural gift. Establishment is about spiritual strength, zeal, vigor, energy and vitality. For a person to receive this kind of impartation they should be found honoring those the Lord has set before them.

> *1 Thessalonians 2:8: "So, affectionately longing for you, we were well pleased to impart to you not only the gospel of God, but also our own lives, because you had become dear to us." (NKJV).*

Here is Paul again, telling his spiritual children in Thessalonica that it was his pleasure to share, give over, transfer, transport, transposition and exchange; not only the gospel, but his very life *(Greek: psuche (psoo-*

khay'), breath, i.e. [by implication] spirit...) to them because he loved them dearly. This is not any different from what Elisha received from Elijah. In Acts 3:6, Peter gave of what he possessed in his spirit. The lame man would not have walked if there was no impartation from Peter.

> Philippians 1:7: *"Even as it is meet for me to think this of you all, because I have you in my heart; in as much as both in my bonds, and in the defense and confirmation of the gospel, ye all are partakers of my grace."* (NKJV)

Philippians 1:1-6 talks about the Philippians honoring Paul through their offerings during his defense and proclamation of the gospel and in his bonds of prison. It was one of the few churches that supported him financially. Against this background is verse 7, where he tells them that because of their giving, they were partakers of and would share in his grace. This is also an inference of impartation. Through their giving, Paul was able to impart his grace to them, giving them access to share it with him.

So, How does Impartation Happen?

Impartation is more effective and beneficial in a spiritual father-son relationship of honor. It is my personal belief that there has to be some kind of relationship for impartation to happen. I don't think it happens to crowds, but to sons, disciples and mentees who are in a relationship with their spiritual father.

The following points are bound by this position:
1) Honor and service
2) Laying on of hands (Deuteronomy 34:9, Acts 6:6; 2 Timothy 1:6)
3) Prophetic ministry (1 Timothy 4:14)
4) Hearing, receiving and taking heed to the gospel with meekness (James 1:21-22)
5) Giving and sowing financial seeds (Philippians 1:3-7)
6) Association: Saul and his servants, although not prophets, prophesied just because they got close and associated with a "company of prophets" (1 Samuel 10:11; 19:24).

The Negative Effects of Impartation

2 Timothy 5:22: "Lay hands suddenly on no man, neither be a partaker of other men's sins: keep thyself pure." (NKJV)

Ephesians 5:7: "Therefore, do not be partakers with them." (NKJV)

2 John 1:11: "For the one who gives him a greeting participates in his evil deeds." (NKJV)

This is very controversial; therefore, I will keep it brief. From the Greek figurative transliteration, impartation can be perverted. That is, in receiving from your spiritual father or the leader you honor and submit to, it is also very easy to unconsciously receive his weaknesses and personal failures. I think that because one might be spending large amounts of time with their spiritual fathers, their weaknesses and failures might become normal in their eyes so it will be very easy for them to practice the same.

Unless one is very alert and spiritually aware, it is easy to pick an ugly habit from your spiritual father. Elisha had an anger problem, just like his spiritual father Elijah. Experience has also proved this point. I have seen spiritual sons exhibiting the same weaknesses and failures like their spiritual fathers. It does happen; sad!!

Contextually speaking, the above verses that I have quoted above are specifically about false and evil brethren, but in them the truth I am discussing is revealed. As we relate, submit, or honor other people, it is very possible to partake of their sins, learn their wickedness, and become participators in their evil deeds. All through the Old and New Testaments, this truth is laid out bare for the sensitive bible student.

Proverbs 22:24-25: "Don't befriend angry people or associate with hot-tempered people, 25 or you will learn to be like them and endanger your soul." (NLT)

1 Corinthians 15:33: "Do not be misled: "Bad company corrupts good character." (NIV)

Psalm 1:1: "Blessed is the man who does not walk in the counsel of the wicked or stand in the way of sinners or sit in the seat of mockers." (NIV)

1 Corinthians 5:11: "But now I am writing you that you must not associate with anyone who calls himself a brother but is sexually immoral or greedy, an idolater or a slanderer, a drunkard or a swindler. With such a man do not even eat." (NIV)

CHAPTER 8

GOD MANIFESTING THROUGH MORTAL MEN

"Men of Israel, listen to this: Jesus of Nazareth was a man accredited by God to you by miracles, wonders and signs, which God did among you through him, as you yourselves know. 23 This man was handed over to you by God's set purpose and foreknowledge; and you, with the help of wicked men, put him to death by nailing him to the cross." [72]

In the grand scheme of things, man is replaceable, dispensable and fallible. His dispensability and fallibility are in terms of God finding another man to use for His purposes. Nevertheless, God still needs a human vessel to fulfill His purposes on earth. Christ was God in a human called Jesus. In Israel, Jesus is a normal name with the same pronunciation and meaning like Joshua. [73]

The exalted Christ we believe and worship today was a man, a son of Joseph. He was totally man and everything He said or did was done like a man in total communion and intimacy with God.

[72] Acts 2:22-23; New International Version

[73] Iesous (ee-ay-sooce'); of Hebrew origin; Jesus (i.e. Jehoshua), the name of our Lord and two (three) other Israelites: (Biblesoft's New Exhaustive Strong's Numbers and Concordance with Expanded Greek-Hebrew Dictionary. Copyright © 1994, 2003, 2006 Biblesoft, Inc. and International Bible Translators, Inc.)

The example of the man Jesus is proof that for God to do anything on earth, He will need to find a humble man willing to be used and possessed by Him. Why would God need man to fulfill and accomplish His purposes on the earth yet He is the one who created it? Psalm 115:16 answers us thus: *"The heaven, even the heavens, are the Lord's; But the earth He has given to the children of men (NKJV)."* Man is the "owner" of the earthly domain, so God cannot just access it without going through man. In the same way, man cannot access heaven without going through God (Christ). Therefore, through His foreknowledge, God chose to manifest Himself through mortal men to accomplish His purposes on earth.

Do Servants of God "Cause" the Miracles, Signs and Wonders they perform?

For purposes of not being misunderstood in this chapter, and also for the purpose of correcting a growing error among Charismatic and Pentecostal circles (especially apostolic and prophetic ministries), allow me to state that although it is evident that it is God who works through His ministers, there is an unconscious tendency by some fanatical believers and ministers to think that servants of God are the cause of the supernatural deeds they do.

Whether it is prophetic gifts, miracles, signs and wonders, generosity, teaching, raising of the dead, or whatever manifestation of the Spirit it might be, servants of God are mere conduits of the manifest presence of God.It does not matter how gifted a servant of God might be, neither they, nor the people around them should ever forget that the source of each manifestation is the Spirit of God, not them.

2 Corinthians 4:7 says: *"But we have this treasure in earthen vessels, that the excellence of the power may be of God and not of us (NKJV)"*. This confirms that the vessel is not the source of the treasure, but God. Instead of giving undue praise and honor to the vessel, all the glory and honor should be unto the Lord who uses the vessel for His purposes. Even if the vessel being used is a "vessel of honor" (2 Timothy 2:20-22), the honor it has is not of itself, but of God who works in it to will and to do for His good pleasure (Philippians 2:13). Whatever is

94

manifested through the vessel is for divine purpose, not for self-glory and gratification.

Acts 10:28 says that it was because of the anointing and Spirit of God upon Christ that He was able to go about doing good, healing all who were possessed by the devil, because God was with Him. Even Christ Himself could not perform the miracles, signs and wonders without the manifest presence of God. Why would a minister or those around them insinuate or allege that it is the vessel that has caused a supernatural occurrence? On our own we can do nothing. We are mere vessels that can be put aside any time.

With that in mind, I shall go ahead to show how God would choose to use certain vessels for His purposes. Throughout the bible, God used various men and women to accomplish His purposes. From Genesis to the present day, we see different human vessels carrying and manifesting the God of the universe. For example:

- **Adam and Eve:** To start the human race, God chose the first couple to reproduce, multiply and fill the earth.

- **Abraham:** To start the nation of Israel God chose Abraham.

- **Moses:** To deliver the children of Israel from Egypt God chose Moses.

- **Aaron:** To start the priesthood ministry, God chose Aaron.

- **Joshua:** To take the children of Israel into the promised land God chose Joshua

- **Joseph:** God chose this Hebrew as the Prime Minister of Egypt, full of wisdom, to store up and manage food to save the then known world from famine.

- **David:** To establish an eternal kingdom, God chose the young shepherd boy after His own heart as a model of what was to come.

- **The 12 Disciples:** For the start and spread of early Christianity from Jerusalem and beyond, God chose these low-class men to start and lead the new movement that would later turn the world upside down.

- **Paul:** For the gospel to reach the gentiles, God called and used a former Pharisee and murderer into the gospel, later sending Him to the gentiles. It was also through Paul that God revealed justification by faith and salvation by grace through faith.

- **William J. Seymour:** Although some small sections in Christianity were receiving the Holy Ghost and speaking in tongues (like the Moravians) before the Azusa street revival, God chose to use the one-eyed face of William J. Seymour to bring this revelation to the forefront.

- **Martin Luther:** For the reformation of Christian theology at that time and the birth of the Protestant faction, God needed this German monk to teach that justification was by faith alone apart from works.

- **Martin Luther King Jr:** God used him to advocate for civil rights and equality for African Americans in the USA. God needed this Baptist preacher and orator to pay the price.

- **David Livingstone and Hudson Taylor:** To popularize oversees missions, God chose David Livingstone to Africa and Hudson Taylor and his China Inland Mission.

- **William Booth:** For God to show that apart from preaching the gospel we also had to care for the needy, God used William Booth, his kitchen soup kiosks and orphanage as examples.

- **Katherine Kuhlman** taught the body of Christ divine healing and the importance of carrying the presence of the Holy Spirit daily. God elevated this blond uneducated girl from Missouri to the world stage.

- **Smith Wigglesworth:** In bringing the gift of faith to the forefront, God used the illiterate Briton, Smith Wigglesworth as its face.

- **Stephen Jeffreys and Alexander Dowie:** God chose to manifest Himself through Jeffery, the Welsh Revivalist in Britain and Alexander Dowie of City of Zion in Illinois, the USA, to bring divine healing to the forefront.

- **Billy Graham, T.L Osborn and Reinhard Bonnke:** God chose these men to popularize global mass evangelism and conversions through powerful crusades.

- **Kenneth Hagin, Oral Roberts and Kenneth Copeland:** The "Word of Faith" movement pushed forward these men and others into the forefront. Through them the church learnt the importance of mixing faith and the Word together to access a miracle. God orchestrated it.

- **William Branham:** God used this man, even though his later years were chaotic, to bring the gift of the "Word of Knowledge" to the forefront.

- **Joseph Prince and Andrew Wommack:** From the Apostle Paul until now, God has been bringing the gospel of Grace to the forefront. For our generation, God chose to use these two men to cure the Body of Christ from legalism.

- **Tony Evans:** To emphasize the importance of families, Tony Evans was called as a face to this core tenet in Christendom.

- **Simeon Kayiwa and Robert Kayanja:** God raised those two men as the face of Pentecostalism in Uganda. The masses associated Pentecostals with those two men and most ministers trace their roots to them.

- **Benson Idahosa:** In Nigeria, God raised up this man as a leading figure in the growth and spread of Pentecostal and charismatic churches. Almost all the elderly ministers of the gospel in Nigeria encountered or sat under this man.

I can go on and on, naming different people, but I guess you notice that for every divine purpose under the sun, God will first look for a man, reveal His will to him, give him access into His mysteries, a platform, resources and fame.

Biblical Perspective

Scriptures have instances that depict how God works through sons(male and female) of men. We shall look at a few of them.

Acts 5:14-16: "And believers were increasingly added to the Lord, multitudes of both men and women, 15 so that they brought the sick out into the streets and laid them on beds and couches, that at least the shadow of Peter passing by might fall on some of them. 16 Also a multitude gathered from the surrounding cities to Jerusalem, bringing sick people and those who were tormented by unclean spirits, and they were all healed." (NKJV) Acts 19:12: "So that even handkerchiefs or aprons were brought from his body to the sick, and the diseases left them and the evil spirits went out of them." (NKJV)

When God chose to manifest Himself through Peter, it was Peter's shadow that healed the sick, not God's shadow. His shadow even "unintentionally" healed because I don't think that he knew everyone to whom his shadow fell upon. The same thing happened with Paul. Handkerchiefs or aprons that came in contact with his body became conduits of the presence and power of God to heal and cast out demons. However, it is important to note that Peter or Paul never "invented" or suggested that people do these things.

It was by the people's own "revelations" that they figured out that Peter's shadow or that aprons and handkerchiefs from Paul healed. This brings us to the next question: If people used objects from Peter and Paul to receive various miracles, does that mean that the people worshiped Peter and Paul? Or does it mean that they worshiped the objects used in receiving from the anointing on the disciples' lives? I don't think so. Why? Because there is that point in the anointing when everything from the minister of the gospel carries that virtue. From that point on, whoever comes in contact with any object from them, is as if they have met the very men and women who carry the anointing because they receive from their gifts the same way they would have received from them physically. Peter and Paul exhibited this kind of manifestation.

> Mark 5:27-28: *"When she heard about Jesus, she came behind Him in the crowd and touched His garment. 28 For she said, "If only I may touch His clothes, I shall be made well." (NKJV)*

When the woman with the issue of blood heard about a man called Jesus and how he had the power to heal, she purposed in her heart to only touch the hem of his garment, believing that she would be healed. This is what she did, and she was totally healed. Jesus was so full of the power of God that even the clothes he wore transferred it to anyone in need. These scriptures in reference show that the miracles depended on the revelation and faith of the people who discerned that they would be healed if they did something physical, not on the carriers of the power.

> 2 Kings 13:21: *"So it was, as they were burying a man, that suddenly they spied a band of raiders; and they put the man in the tomb of Elisha; and when the man was let down and touched the bones of Elisha, he revived and stood on his feet." (NKJV)*

Elisha died with his anointing because he had not been able to pass it down like Elijah did with him. If Gehazi, Elisha's would-be-heir, had not forfeited spiritual laws, he would have carried over a fourth portion of the anointing of Elisha. As we increase our awareness of the presence of God, as we continue to exercise this presence on a daily basis and learn and mature in appropriating this presence for every situation, there comes a time when the divine unction saturates every bone, sinew, fiber, blood and our entire bodies that everything and everyone that comes in contact with us is affected by it.

This is what we learn from the above scriptures we have referenced:

- The one with a need determines how they approach the one who has the spiritual solution. It should not be the other way around. It is a personal revelation of HOW you receive from a gift on a someone's life. There is no rule to this.
- The power, anointing, or working of miracle is not in the object, it is in the Spirit upon the man or woman. The objects act as "points of contact", but those "points of contact" should never become idols to be worshiped or formulas and methods. God cannot be limited and boxed into objects.
- We cannot approach or discern ministers of God, or have a revelation of access into the miraculous if we do not honor the men and women that God has set before us.

Integrating Honor in the Five-Fold Gifts

Various theological debates and disagreements surround what has been termed as the "five-fold" gifts of ministry. The opponents say the gifts distributed by the glorified Christ listed in Ephesians 4:11-13 ceased and they are no longer active. Proponents say Christ still gives gifts to some to be apostles, prophets, evangelists, pastors and teachers.

> **"The power, anointing, or working of miracle is not in the object, it is in the Spirit upon the man or woman"**

I am not a ceaseationist, so I will go ahead and advocate for the operation of these "offices" in the body of Christ because those in church leadership normally fall under these gifts and callings. We honor them because God has set them over us, but we first need a spiritual understanding of who they are and how they function.

The advancement of the idea of "five-fold" ministerial gifts stems from the book of Ephesians 4:11-13. In that chapter, you will not find the term "Five-Fold", but you will find a set of five gifts distributed by the resurrected and glorified Christ. Paul, writing by inspiration of the Holy Spirit, also outlines the functions of these men [and women]. This is how the portion of that scripture reads:

> " **We honor them because God has set them over us, but we first need a spiritual understanding of who they are and how they function** "

And He Himself gave some to be apostles, some prophets, some evangelists, and some pastors and teachers, 12 for the equipping of the saints for the work of ministry, for the edifying of the body of Christ, 13 till we all come to the unity of the faith and of the knowledge of the Son of God, to a perfect man, to the measure of the stature of the fullness of Christ. (NKJV)

So, this scripture outlines apostles, prophets, evangelists, pastors and teachers who Christ gives gifts to equip the saints for the work of the ministry and to edify and build His body. The purpose of these gifts is to equip the Body for the work of the ministry and also edify her until we will all come to the unity of the faith (with no divisions in what we believe even though we may have different denominations). We will grow in the knowledge of the Son of God, and we will become perfect according the measure of the stature of the fullness of Christ.

A brief review in the Strong's Hebrew and Greek Definitions[74] reveal the nature and functions of these men [and women].

---

[74] Biblesoft's New Exhaustive Strong's Numbers and Concordance with Expanded Greek-Hebrew Dictionary. Copyright © 1994, 2003, 2006 Biblesoft, Inc. and International Bible Translators, Inc.

Apostle: (apostolos (ap-os'-tol-os): A delegate; specially an ambassador of the Gospel; officially a commissioner of Christ ["apostle"] (with miraculous powers). Their functions include **Governing**, pioneering new work and laying foundations, equipping and perfecting the saints, establishing sound doctrine and revelation. He also sets local assemblies in order as he or she raises sons and daughters in the Lord. They create a supernatural culture.

Prophet: (prophetes (prof-ay'-tace): A foreteller ("prophet"). He is an inspired speaker by analogy and a poet by extension. Functions include: **Guiding**, Spiritual sight, edification, comforting, foretelling, forth telling and execution of a supernatural culture.

Evangelist: (euaggelistes (yoo-ang-ghel-is-tace'): This is a preacher of the gospel. Some of his functions include **Gathering**, proclaiming, mass conversions, miracles, signs and wonders - especially healing.

Pastor: (poimen (poy-mane'): He is a shepherd (literally or figuratively). His functions include **Guarding**, feeding, caring, tending and protecting the flock.

Teacher: (didaskalos (did-as'-kal-os): An instructor (genitive case or specially). This includes, but is not limited to **Growing**, instructing, teaching, discipling and correcting the saints.

It is important to note that there has to be teamwork for any of the five-fold ministerial gifts to function effectively. The New Testament reveals that the Apostle Paul rarely moved alone. He was always in the company of other people. I think that his teams involved apostles, prophets, evangelists, shepherds and teachers working with him. The corporate functioning of the five-fold gifts will result in Ephesians 4:13 – where every person has been perfected unto the measure of the stature of the fullness of Christ. Working in isolation or suppressing other gifts and elevating others is one of the reasons Christ has not yet returned. His Bride has not yet been perfected by the five-fold gifts because many of them are busy building their own kingdoms in isolation of one another. One out of the five-fold gifts cannot perfect the body of Christ alone. All the gifts need to work in cooperation.[75] In His book, "Culture of Honor; Sustaining a Supernatural Culture", Danny Silk says: "I am convinced that one of the reasons senior church leaders experience the disheartening cycle of great outpourings that gradually return to business as usual is a lack of understanding of the fivefold ministry, of their own ministry anointings and callings, and of how their anointings shape the direction of their churches."[76]

Apostles and Prophets

In the Old Testament, it was the prophets that led the spiritual life of the children of Israel. They prophesied and wrote the different books in the Old Testament. In the New Testament, we see apostles taking the lead from the day of Pentecost to the time of the Roman invasion of AD 70. They also wrote the different books we have of the New Testament. In the fourth century, the Roman Empire declared freedom of worship. From this development, new leadership forms and structures that were not found in the New Testament began to form from within the Catholic Church. This partly led to the confusion in church leadership today.

From the reformation to Protestantism, many other factions and denominations sprang up from the Anglican Church. The Anglican Church had adopted most of the forms of the Catholic Church. In trying to move back to the New Testament church, the Evangelicals (Charismatics and Pentecostals included) broke away from the main Protestant denominations to start their own. However, since they also lacked a deeper revelation of the New Testament model, the average Evangelical church teaches, forexample, that apostles should not lead local congregations. They say the apostle's work is limited to planting, equipping and setting up pastors over the church. To this end, prophets are persecuted (due to their own or other people's failures). To flee the

---

[75] "The Church Life Model: A Biblical Pattern For The Spirit-Filled Church." Creation House, 2011; by Wayne and Sherry Lee is a great resource for local assemblies that want to implement a 5 Fold Ministerial functions model in their congregations. I highly recommend it

[76] Danny Silk. Culture of Honor: Sustaining a Supernatural Environment (Kindle Locations 441-443). Destiny Image. Kindle Edition.

hostility, they leave local assemblies to start their own *para* ministries. In the end, the local church is only led by pastors, teachers, administrators or evangelists. Without the full functioning of the five-fold ministry, a supernatural environment cannot be created and sustained in our congregations. There is also no manifestation of the fullness of Christ through believers, thus hindering the Kingdom of heaven from invading the earth.

1 Corinthians 12:28 says: *"And God has appointed these in the church: first apostles, second prophets, third teachers, after that miracles, then gifts of healings, helps, administrations, varieties of tongues (NKJV)."* This should prove to us that God's design for leadership within the Body in a local assembly is one led by apostles and prophets. It should not have only pastors, teachers or administrators as is the norm today. Dany Silk further says:

"Paul clearly lays out an order of priority in this passage, and this order is related to the realms of the supernatural that correspond to each particular office. The anointing on the apostle and prophet creates a perspective that is primarily focused on perceiving what is going on in Heaven and bringing that to earth. The teacher is focused on being able to describe everything that happened accurately, and the evangelist and pastor are focused on the people." [77]

Allowing apostles and prophets to take the lead in the core leadership teams in local congregations in the body of Christ will enhance a supernatural atmosphere.[78] It will restore what is lacking in the church (Ephesians 4:13) and then Christ will return for His perfected Bride. There is more on this we can learn from the bible.

Acts 13:1: "Now in the church that was at Antioch there were certain prophets and teachers: Barnabas, Simeon who was called Niger, Lucius of Cyrene, Manaen who had been brought up with Herod the tetrarch, and Saul." (NKJV)

---

[77] Danny Silk. Culture of Honor: Sustaining a Supernatural Environment (Kindle Locations 564-567). Destiny Image. Kindle Edition.
[78] Acts 5:12

Ephesians 2:19-22: "Now, therefore, you are no longer strangers and foreigners, but fellow citizens with the saints and members of the household of God, 20 having been built on the foundation of the apostles and prophets, Jesus Christ Himself being the chief cornerstone, 21 in whom the whole building, being fitted together, grows into a holy temple in the Lord, 22 in whom you also are being built together for a dwelling place of God in the Spirit." (NKJV)

It seems that apostles and prophetic teachers were quite plenty at Antioch. They were so many that the Holy Spirit had to hand-pick Barnabas and Saul for the work He had set for them, otherwise all the other apostles and prophetic-teachers would have presented themselves! The increase in number of these apostles and prophetic-teachers was as a result of the extensive equipping of the saints through teaching[79] that Barnabas and Saul had been doing for a year. Apostles and prophets have the supernatural ability to equip, nature and perfect the saints to become Christ-like. That is probably why believers were first called Christians at Antioch; further leading to the rise of apostles and prophetic-teachers in this local assembly.

Ephesians 2:20 points out that the Ekklesia of Christ is built on the foundation of apostles and prophets. It is easy to think that Paul is talking about Old Testament prophets and New Testament apostles as the foundation of the church. That is not so, otherwise the ordering of the words would have been prophets and apostles. Paul further said everyone should build on their foundation. No wonder he calls himself a wise master-builder.[80] In verse 21, the apostles and prophets build the saints into a dwelling place of God in the Spirit. They also do the fitting together of the whole building, bringing all the spiritual nuts and bolts together into a complete structure. The strength of the building is determined by the strength of the foundation. Strong assemblies require strong leaders and apostles and prophets provide that stability. In their book, "The Church Life Model: A Biblical Pattern For The Spirit-Filled Church" Wayne and Sherry Lee say:

---

[79] Acts 11:25-26
[80] Romans 15:20; 1 Corinthians 3:10-12

105

The role of the apostolic function, however, often causes misgivings for those who take issue with identifying any leaders as apostles. We certainly believe that caution is warranted in this matter. However, the apostolic role signals strong giftings in both leadership and management. Leaders who manifest the apostolic function in the areas of missionary work and church planting seem reasonable to most and enjoy acceptance. We would contend, however, that the apostolic function was given to the church just as the role-gifts of pastor, teacher, or evangelist.[81]

Just like Wayne and Sherry Lee say, the traditional understanding and function of the apostles has been outside local assemblies than in the day-to-day leading of congregations of believers. It is the general, but unofficial consensus that anyone claiming to be an apostle should be planting churches and doing missions in unreached areas. On the other hand, they are considered idle and redundant if they attend an organized congregation of believers. But research (from Wayne and Lee's book) has proved that people with an apostolic role and anointing possess entrepreneurial and managerial leadership skills to lead others.

> **Apostles and prophets do not lead in a top-down hierarchy, but rather, in a "coach-football team" kind of structure**

They also have supernatural skills that work well in local assemblies, leading to the growth of the congregation.

In advocating for apostolic leaders to lead core teams, Danny Silk gives more insight into this:

Apostolic leaders are focused on Heaven, and their mission is to see Heaven's supernatural reality established on the earth. They long to see the evidence of Heaven's touch in the environment they lead or influence.

[81] Lee, Wayne and Sherry. The Church Life Model: A Biblical Pattern For The Spirit-Filled Church. Creation House. 2011. Illustrated Edition. pp 35-36

Having this motivation at the foundation of a church leads to an entirely different emphasis in the church's governing priorities. The apostle will make the presence of God, the worship of God, and the agenda of Heaven the top priorities in the environment. An apostolic government is designed to protect these priorities.[82]

And on prophets, he says:

We need someone to keep us expectant and aware of the ever-present reality of the Kingdom. Apostles keep us believing, but prophets keep us expecting that God is coming. The dynamic ways in which God speaks to the prophet, including dreams, visions, and trances, create awareness of God's involvement with us. These supernatural tools introduce an infusion of sensitivity toward heaven's activity and plans.[83]

Apostles and prophets should not lead in a top-down hierarchy, but rather, in a "coach-football team" kind of structure. The apostles' vision of heaven being realized on the earth, the prophets' role of creating an awareness and expectation for heaven's invasion on the earth through the Body of Christ and the evangelists' zeal to take heaven outside of the Body of Christ to the lost must all work hand-in-hand with the pastor's role of caring for the Body and the teacher's role of teaching the Body.

All these callings work together to set up believers as a force to reckon with. It is my personal belief that all the other gifts still fall under the "five-fold" gifts of Ephesians 4:11-13. I think that each believer in the Body of Christ is either apostolic, prophetic, evangelistic, pastoral or an instructor; who all just need discipleship and mentoring to grow in "full" fivefold. Because of that belief, we can place each of the gifts listed in Romans 12:6-8, 1 Corinthians 12:8-10 and 1 Peter 4:11 under the main" five-fold" Gifts. The more the "five-fold" ministers equip the saints for the work of ministry and build the body of Christ, the more believers will mature into core "five-fold" leaders who will in turn lead other saints into becoming core leaders and the cycle will continue. The following figures illustrate this belief.

[82] Danny Silk. Culture of Honor: Sustaining a Supernatural Environment (Kindle Locations 638-642). Destiny Image. Kindle Edition
[83] Ibid. Kindle Locations 708-711.

Figure 1: "Five-Fold" Ministry Operation

The figure above shows us that God is at the center of the Body, supplying the core team of apostles, prophets, evangelists, pastors and teachers with vision, grace, faith and the anointing to function in the five-fold gifts. And as they "equip the saints for the work of ministry", the saints are also supplied with vision, grace, faith, and the anointing to function in their gifts.

Figure 2: "Five-fold" leadership perspective

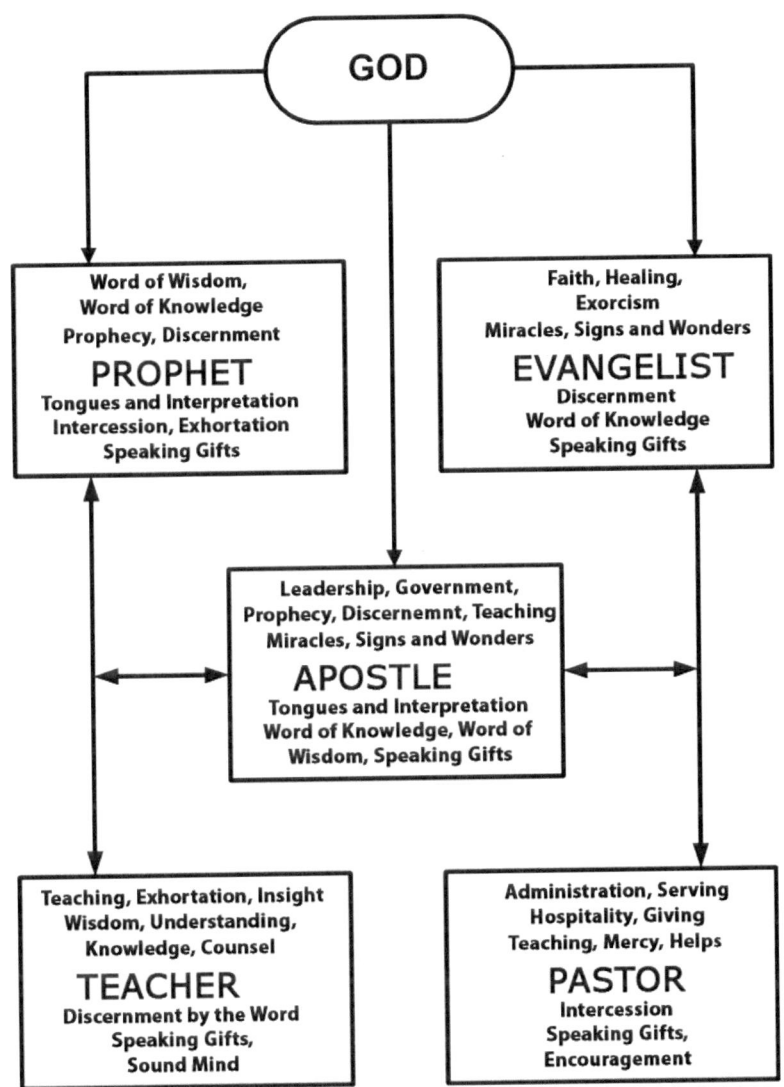

From the above figure we learn that God is the ultimate leader. He leads through "the foundation of apostles and prophets." The apostle is the leader of the core team, guiding other "five-fold" leaders as they encourage other gifted believers into spiritual growth, maturity and the execution of their gifts and callings.

Note: As we move into the last of the last days, we are going to see more and more apostles and prophets rise from different parts of the world. They shall mostly rise from Africa, South America and Asia. As they go out in faith and authority, they will shake the fabric of twisted beliefs and understanding of spiritual gifts, the operation of God's Spirit and the supernatural realm. As this is going on, there will also be a raising of the sons of the devil, who will also not be easily discerned.

The New Testament church must operate in kingdom honor. This will help the "five-fold" ministry to function as a team in a peaceful, healthy and non-competitive manner. Silk elaborates on this by saying that;

"When five-fold leaders model this kind of honor amongst themselves, then "equipping the saints" becomes a matter of extending honor by releasing every individual believer into his or her unique identity and destiny. Each believer comes to understand his or her significance in relationship to the whole Body, and the conviction begins to take hold: "I carry something that no one else carries. I must develop and release my gifts into the Church and the world and do my part in bringing Heaven to earth." Honor empowers people." [84]

When we live and practice the kingdom culture of honoring one another, each one of us will be empowered to fulfill their God-given visions, dreams and purposes. When this happens, conflicts, fights, competition and church politics will become history, because everyone will know their abilities and graces while honoring and appreciating the diversity in others that are gifted differently.

The Principle of Honor

Danny Silk introduces what he calls, "The Principle of Honor", which states that: *"Accurately acknowledging who people are will position us to give them what they deserve and to receive the gift of who they are in our lives."*[85]

---

[84] Danny Silk. Culture of Honor: Sustaining a Supernatural Environment (Kindle Locations 828-832). Destiny Image. Kindle Edition.
[85] Ibid. Kindle Locations 184-185

From this principle, I can assert that: we cannot receive from people's gifts and callings if we do not honorably acknowledge those gifts and callings.

Our reception depends on how we honor people irrespective of their social standing, economic status, or where they were born. Everyone deserves our unreserved acknowledgement and honor to reach their full potential.

It is my desire that the body of Christ lives in honor with one another. The next chapter will show us how to do this.

"Therefore, indeed, I send you prophets, wise men, and scribes: some of them you will kill and crucify, and some of them you will scourge in your synagogues and persecute from city to city."
Matthew 23:34, NKJV

CHAPTER 9

BIBLICAL EXPRESSIONS OF HONOR

"In Jewish tradition, Abraham, the ancestor of the Jews, was an example of an honorable man who could rightly claim honor ("boast", Romans 4:2). But not so, according to Paul: Abraham remained the honorable man and an example for all believers, but he could not claim any honor of his own making; his status rested solely on grace and on the promise of God (Romans 4:16)" [86]

In December 2016, photos of the minister of Sports and Physical Education in Cameroon surfaced on mainstream and social media showing him greeting his president with a sharp bow, stretching his hand to shake the president's at a distance. The minister was bashed, poked, and made fun of because of his respectful gesture towards his president. Furthermore, various memes were created to stretch the fun further. Society currently frowns at "strange" expressions of honor. However, what does the Bible say about representations, expressions, and manifestations of honor? The results will shock you. There cannot be true honor (whether as a noun or verb) without a representation, manifestation or expression of glory.

---

[86] Moxnes, Halvor; Honor and Shame: An Essay, University of Oslo, Page 11

Some examples of the expression of glory include wealth, reputation, majesty, splendor, influence, gifts, reverence, excellence, heaviness (of something), weightiness, respect, relationships, position, humility, submission, power and authority. We see representations, manifestations and expressions of honor from different people towards one another in the bible. Scriptures teach us that honor is esteeming and preferring others better than ourselves (Philippians 2:3-4). True honor comes from humility and selflessness.

The first representations, manifestations and expressions of honor in the Old Testament show us that honor was always expressed physically and in visible ways. The person giving honor always did something that showed that they truly revered those they thought should be honored. There were no laws, rules, regulations or guidelines to these representations, manifestations and expressions. People chose how to honor those they thought should be honored. Let us look at some scriptures that illustrate this.

Genesis 23:7: *"Then Abraham rose and bowed down before the people of the land, the Hittites." (NKJV)*
The very first-time scriptures show representations, manifestations and expressions of honor is through "bowing down" to the ground before the person to whom the honor was due. Of course, there was also a cultural aspect to this expression because of the cultures of the Ancient Near East (ANE[87]) nations at that time.

The ANE had its unique ways in which they practiced and lived in honor with one another. We see Abraham, the father of nations, blessed by God, bowing down before the Hittites, a "heathen" nation that generations later Israel would conquer and dislodge. However, Abraham had to honor them as he spoke to them about buying a burial ground for his family (Sarah had just died).

[87]The Ancient Near East was the home of early civilizations within a region roughly corresponding to the modern Middle East: Mesopotamia (modern Iraq, southeast Turkey, southwest Iran, northeastern Syria and Kuwait),ancient Egypt, ancient Iran (Elam, Media, Parthia and Persia), Anatolia/Asia Minor and Armenian Highlands (Turkey's Eastern Anatolia Region, Armenia, northwestern Iran, southern Georgia, and western Azerbaijan),the Levant (modern Syria, Lebanon, Palestine, Israel, and Jordan), Cyprus and the Arabian Peninsula. (Wikipedia: Ancient Near East (11/09/2018), retrieved from https://en.wikipedia.org/wiki/Ancient_Near_East on 20/09/2018 at 5:55am)

The Easton's Bible Dictionary defines Bowing as: "…a mode of showing respect. Abraham "bowed himself to the people of the land" (Genesis 23:7); also, Jacob to Esau (Genesis 33:3); and the brethren of Joseph before him as the governor of the land (Genesis 43:28). Bowing is also frequently mentioned as an act of adoration to idols (Joshua 23:7; 2 Kings 5:18; Judges 2:19; Isaiah 44:15), and to God (Joshua 5:14; Psalms 22:29; 72:9; Micah 6:6; Psalms 95:6; Ephesians 3:14).

It is evident through Easton's Bible Dictionary's definition that bowing down[88] was an act of honor either to other men, idols, kings, or the God of Israel. What gave meaning to this act of honor was the person who carried it out. They determined who or what to give it to and the kind of "honor-act" that would best describe what they felt about that person or object.

Gen 33:3-8: Then he crossed over before them and bowed himself to the ground seven times, until he came near to his brother. 4 But Esau ran to meet him, and embraced him, and fell on his neck and kissed him, and they wept. 5 And he lifted his eyes and saw the women and children, and said, "Who are these with you?" So he said, "The children whom God has graciously given your servant." 6 Then the maidservants came near, they and their children, and bowed down. 7 And Leah also came near with her children, and they bowed down. Afterward Joseph and Rachel came near, and they bowed down. 8 Then Esau said, "What do you mean by all this company which I met?" And he said, "These are to find favor in the sight of my lord (NKJV).

The above scripture shows Jacob bowing down seven times until he approached his brother Esau. Just imagine that! Bowing down seven times until you meet the one before whom you seek favor! Esau did not find this necessary, but he also did not stop his brother from doing so. He, on the other hand, ran towards him, embraced and kissed him (this was also a sign of honor and a form of greeting in the ANE nations at that time). Jacob was not the only one bowing before Esau, but also his wives, concubines and children. Basically, the entire family

---
[88] Some more scriptures from Jesus' time on earth; Luke 8:41-42; Luke 17:15-16; John 11:32

115

bowed before this man who had lost his birthright. Esau had lost his blessing and the opportunity to become a descendant of Jesus Christ. Yet Jacob, the one who had the birthright and the blessing, together with his family, bowed down before Esau because they sought to obtain favor before him.

The argument that Jacob was trying to bribe Esau again by bowing down to him does not add up because by the 33rd chapter of Genesis, Jacob had already encountered God in chapter 32 and his life had been transformed (God had already given him a new name to that effect). By the time he meets Esau, the gifts Jacob had sent earlier were not to bribe his brother, but to give him access so that he could find favor before him. Giving of gifts was also a cultural practice of honor in the ANE. You could not meet a person you esteemed as great or sought audience with without a gift in your hand.

> *Gen 41:43: "And he had him ride in the second chariot which he had; and they cried out before him, "Bow the knee!" So he set him over all the land of Egypt." (NKJV).*

> *Gen 42:6: "Now Joseph was governor over the land; and it was he who sold to all the people of the land. And Joseph's brothers came and bowed down before him with their faces to the earth." (NKJV).*

> *Gen 43:28: "They replied, "Your servant our father is still alive and well." And they bowed low to pay him honor." (NIV).*

These verses are extracted from a story about Joseph when he had just been appointed Prime Minister of Egypt. Wherever Joseph went, the Egyptians bowed their knees before him because it was a sign of honor to those in political authority. Sometime later, Joseph's brothers also came to Egypt to buy wheat because of the severe famine that had covered the then known world. They bowed down with their faces to the ground (also in fulfillment of his dreams) because they had to honor this Egyptian prince who had the authority to deny or sell them food. After they got to know that it was Joseph their brother they were dumbfounded.

When he inquired about the state of his father Jacob, his brothers referred to him (Jacob) as Joseph's servant, and while doing so, they still bowed down to the earth before Joseph, just as he had dreamt 13 years before. They bowed before him because of the authority, position and respect he commanded in Egypt. The biological relationship they had with him did not matter at that time because of where he was in terms of authority, position and power. Joseph's authority was second only to the Pharaoh; therefore, honor was due to him.

Ruth 2:10: "So she fell on her face, bowed down to the ground, and said to him, "Why have I found favor in your eyes, that you should take notice of me, since I am a foreigner?" (NKJV)

In the Old Testament, whenever anyone came before a person of repute, wealth or majesty, the only way they would obtain favor before those people of repute was through acts of honor. Bowing down, at that time, was a high act of honor one would give to those they esteemed highly. When such an act was expressed, the one expressing it obtained favor before the one they sought it from.

Sometimes, honor was given after favor was received by the one who sought for it. The one who obtained favor would choose to do anything as a sign of honor and gratitude in return for the favor they had received. Whatever such a person chose as an act of honor, there was no law prohibiting them from doing so or choosing that kind of gesture.

Isaiah 49:23: "Kings will be your foster fathers, and their queens your nursing mothers. They will bow down before you with their faces to the ground; they will lick the dust at your feet. Then you will know that I am the Lord; those who hope in me will not be disappointed." (NIV)
Isaiah 60:14: "Also the sons of those who afflicted you Shall come bowing to you, and all those who despised you shall fall prostrate at the soles of your feet; And they shall call you The City of the Lord, Zion of the Holy One of Israel (NKJV)."

1 Samuel 25:23-24,27, 41: "When Abigail saw David, she quickly got off her donkey and bowed down before David with her face to the ground. 24 She fell at his feet and said: "My lord, let the blame be on me alone. Please let your servant speak to you; hear what your servant has to say. 27 And let this gift, which your servant has brought to my master, be given to the men who follow you. 41 She bowed down with her face to the ground and said, "Here is your maidservant, ready to serve you and wash the feet of my master's servants (NIV)."

Luke 7:38: … "and stood at His feet behind Him weeping; and she began to wash His feet with her tears, and wiped them with the hair of her head; and she kissed His feet and anointed them with the fragrant oil."

Some representations, manifestations and expressions of honor in the bible would be offensive to some people in this corporate era of "first-name-basis" meet-ups. That said, scriptures are filled with instances where the highest form of honor was to prostate at someone's feet. In Hebrew culture and the ANE, washing of feet was a gesture of humility and was "officially" done by servants to their masters or his visitors. However, anyone who wanted to show honor and humility of the highest form did it through prostrating or washing of the feet of those they esteemed highly. Jesus shocked his disciples when He, as their master and teacher, laid down his garments, girded himself with a towel, poured water in a basin and washed their feet. He went ahead to wipe them with the towel. This happened after he had learned that the Father had given Him all things and that He was going back to Him (John 13:1-17).

Isaiah Chapter 49 is about the LORD returning and restoring Israel as a nation. It also talks about the adoption of sons and the expansion of the influence and dominance of Zion. It is important to note that, although Israel is the physical nation of the Hebrews, Zion, for the ardent bible scholar, is always a metaphoric and prophetic representation of the church. As the LORD glorifies and expands Zion, sons and daughters are born unto her from around the kingdoms (political spheres) of the world. Kings become foster fathers and queens become nursing mothers to Zion's adopted children (meaning that the true parents of the believer in any nation is the Ekklesia. Politicians are just custodians).

However, because kings and queens understand the diplomacy of kingdoms and how "lesser" kings ought to honor greater kings, they do things differently. As they appear before Zion, bringing back her sons and daughters, the LORD promises that "They will bow down before you with their faces to the ground; they will lick the dust at your feet." God uses a known practice of honor to prophesy the glory of His Kingdom over the kingdoms of this world. The following prophetic interpretations and insights from Isaiah 49:23 and Isaiah 60:14 are worth noting.

1) As the LORD exalts and glorifies the church, nations, kings and queens (politicians and people of repute) will bow down for her sons and daughters (because the church is the people, not buildings and institutions).

2) It is the state that should consult and serve the interests of the church, not vice-versa. (This point does not in any way advocate for state religions like what Christianity became in the days of Emperor Constantine).

3) In the eyes of God, the church has more glory and position than the state, and whenever the LORD looks at any nation, His eyes are always on the church, because the church is the signet of His love and the embodiment of His glory.

4) Apart from the LORD elevating the church corporately, He also elevates and lifts up certain individuals for the furtherance of His Kingdom's influence on the earth. These are the apostles, prophets, evangelists, pastors and teachers.

5) Before God, an apostle, prophet, evangelist, pastor, or teacher of the word in a nation holds more influence over the people than a politician. Even if it does not physically appear so, that is how it should be according to the order of God. Those are the "priests" and "princes" of that nation.

1 Samuel chapter 25 has a story about three people: Nabal, Abigail and David. After the death of Samuel, David moved to the desert of Maon. Nabal, a wealthy, but foolish, surly and mean man was in the same area shearing sheep. The fact that David had treated Nabal's servants and their animals with honor, he thought Nabal would be kind enough to return the favor in form of supplies that he needed to feed his army. When David sent his servants to Nabal, he despised David, calling him Saul's run-away servant. He refused to give him anything, sending David's servants away empty handed. Abigail, Nabal's beautiful and wise wife, heard that David was planning an attack on their camp as a retaliation for being treated badly. She organized two hundred loaves of bread, two skins of wine, five dressed sheep, five seahs[89] of roasted grain, one hundred cakes of raisins and two hundred cakes of pressed figs. She loaded them on donkeys to present them to David as gifts and supplies for his army.

When Abigail saw David from afar off approaching with his men, she climbed down the donkey, fell on her face and bowed down to the ground before him. She perceived that God was with David and that he would become king over Israel with a lasting dynasty (prophesying Christ). She asked him to forgive her and Nabal for his folly. She advised David not to avenge himself by killing Nabal (which would save David's conscience later). She asked him to accept her gifts, and to also spare her when he became king. David was impressed by this woman's counsel (and beauty of course). He accepted her gifts and spared Nabal's camp. After Nabal's death (not at David's hand), David sent emissaries to ask for Abigail's hand in marriage. She accepted the proposal by bowing with her face to the ground while at the same time pledging to serve and wash the feet of David's servants.

It is amazing how differently Nabal and Abigail dealt with David. One in dishonor and the other in honor. Abigail knew what honor was and how to show it. It was all about the perception of who David was and what he meant to each of them. Abigail shows us that people

[89] Wikipedia; (8 June 2017); SEAH (UNIT) ... The se'ah or seah (Hebrew: סאה) is a unit of dry measure of ancient origin used in Halakha (Jewish law), which equals one third of an ephah, or bath. Its size in modern units varies widely according to the criteria used for defining it. Retrieved from https://en.wikipedia.org/wiki/Seah_(unit) at 6:56pm on 15/09/2018

will do anything in honor to the one God has blessed, destined for greatness and exalted. Nabal shows us that it does not matter how honorable a person might be to other people, some people will always be indifferent and callous in their response to that person. Favor is not necessarily reciprocated.

If we lived in the days of Jesus, what would have been our reaction to both Jesus and the harlot who kissed His feet, washed them with her tears, wiped them with her hair and anointed them with the best perfume of the land? I don't think that our reaction would have been any different from Jesus' host at that dinner table where this "drama" was unfolding. Some argue that Mary did that because Jesus is God, but scriptures don't say that at all. On the contrary, scriptures prove that almost all those that dealt with Jesus while on earth dealt with him strictly on two fronts; as a man and as a prophet.

This is what Luke 7:39 proves: *"When the Pharisee who had invited him saw this, he said to himself, "If this man were a prophet, he would know who is touching him and what kind of woman she is — that she is a sinner (NIV)."* Among Jesus' disciples, it is only Peter who got a revelation that Jesus was the Messiah. There was also another occasion in Matthew 17 when God approved the Son before Peter, James and John on the mount of transfiguration and Peter discerned Him. Jesus deliberately hid His divinity from most people. The Pharisee invited a man that he was not even sure was a prophet. Mary honored the man called Jesus. She did not even know that what she was doing was actually preparing Jesus for his burial. Harlots and tax collectors knew how and who to honor, yet Pharisees and the most pious and religious people missed it.

Honor in Eight Dimensions

2 Samuel 16:4: *"And Ziba said, "I humbly bow before you, that I may find favor in your sight, my lord, O king!"* This verse is taken from a very interesting chapter from the book of 2 Samuel chapter 16. I call it "honor in 8 D", because it has eight characters and lessons on honor worth noting.

The first character is Ziba, a "male nanny" of Mephibosheth,

Jonathan's son. Ziba was initially King Saul's servant. He met King David, who was on the run from his son Absalom. Absalom had organized a coup d'é·tat against his father. Ziba had a couple of donkeys, 200 loaves of bread, 100 clusters of raisins, 100 hundred summer fruits and a skin of wine (2 Samuel 16:1-4). Just imagine the time that Ziba took to gather this stuff. These were supplies that Ziba perceived David would need on his journey while running away from Absalom. Ziba honored King David with the gifts he gave him for his journey.

Then there is Mephibosheth, who was in Jerusalem wishing, confessing and declaring that the Kingdom of Israel be restored to the house of his grandfather Saul the day the coup took place. Prior to this, in 2 Samuel 9, David had restored Mephibosheth and gave him everything that belonged to the house of Saul his grandfather. David did this for the sake of Mephibosheth's father Jonathan, David's best friend. Mephibosheth was crippled. He lived at a one Makir's house in a place called Lo DeBar. David gave him access to the king's table, at the palace in Jerusalem. However, the moment he heard that David had been dislodged by his son Absalom, he jubilated. He forgot everything David had done for him. This means that all the prostrations he made before King David as acts of honor when he appeared before him were fake. He never meant anything, but only wanted to survive. Mephibosheth was a selfish schema and an opportunist who knew how to play his way into high places or before great people. He faked honor to get where he wanted to go.

> **Harlots and tax collectors knew how and who to honor, yet Pharisees and the most pious and religious people missed it**

The third character is Shimei, also from Saul's family. When he heard that

David was on the run, he went out and hurled curses at him. He judged and condemned David, accusing him of blackmail. He called him names and threw stones at him. Shimei even had the audacity to speak in the name of God, saying God was repaying David for causing evil and bloodshed in the house of Saul. Shimei was like the devil himself to David, because he became his accuser. He also misinterpreted Absalom's treason, betrayal and abuse of his father's kindness and forgiveness (remember he had murdered Amnon his half-brother for raping Tamar his sister (all David's children from different women}, but David had forgiven him and allowed him to return to Jerusalem). Shimei did not honor the man that had "fallen" from his "ministry" (the throne and kingdom altogether).

Our fourth character is Abishai, one of David's soldiers who did not defect to Absalom's side. However, he betrayed David's honor by cursing and slandering Shimei by calling him a dead dog. Abishai was willing to cut off Shime's head if David gave him permission. Both men operated from the same spirit of dishonor, for if Abishai walked and practiced honor, he would have acted like David towards Shimei.

David is our fifth character because of his response to Abishai and Shimei. In 2 Samuel 16:10 (NIV) David asked Abishai what he had in common with him. That means that they operated from different spirits (one of honor, another of dishonor). That said, I think that in verse 10, David also misinterpreted Shimei's evil to mean God's discipline. This means that David wasn't sure if it was God doing these things or not. David did not think of repaying Shimei for his evil towards him, but left him in the hands of God. He hoped that, God's goodness would come out of the cursing he had received that day. David honored Shimei by not repaying evil-for-evil and Abishai by lovingly rebuking, correcting and turning him away from cutting off Shimei's head.

Our sixth character is Hushai, David's friend who pretended to defect to Absalom's camp. He went to Absalom, hailed and paid homage to him as king. Absalom was shocked because he knew Hushai was his father's friend so he asked him whether that was the love he could show towards his friend and why he did not go with David. Hushai told Absalom that he was his friend and would serve him because he had been chosen by God. Hushai honored his friendship with David through his willingness to enter the enemy's camp and downplay and dislodge Ahithophel's counsel to delay Absalom's attack, so that David would have time to regroup. Loyalty at whatever cost is a true manifestation of honor in relationships.

Ahithophel is our seventh character. He was a very wise and brilliant man. He served David as a senior advisor/consultant to the king. Ahithophel's advice and counsel was equated to inquiring of God. Everybody in Israel trusted and relied on his counsel. At this time, he had defected to Absalom's camp. When they approached Jerusalem, Absalom consulted with Ahithophel about what they should do. Unfortunately, Ahithopel was already out of God's covering and will. He gave Absalom one of the craziest, weirdest and most bizarre advices I have ever heard! He advised Absalom to sleep with his father's concubines who David had left to take care of the palace! Ahithophel's advice worked, because Absalom's company pitched a tent on top of the roof of the palace, in which he slept with David's concubines in the sight of all Israel! Ahithophel dishonored his friend David when he advised Absalom to sleep with his concubines. This was an abomination in Israel. For Absalom to do it in broad daylight made it all the eviler.

The final and eighth character is Absalom himself; the rebel and traitor, who had been David's dishonorable son from the very beginning. In addition to assassinating his half-brother Amnon for raping his sister, he once set Joab (one of David's general)'s farm on fire. He negatively influenced the Israelites when he asked them to consult with him instead of going to the palace. Absalom thereby lured the people's hearts to himself, which was akin to leading a rebel outfit to topple David's kingship. He slept with his father's concubines before all Israel! Absalom dealt dishonorably with the different people he came across, but most especially his father. Absalom represents vengeful, malicious, non-forgiving people. They destroy what is not theirs. They are unruly, selfish and ambitious. They are peace-breakers, envious and blackmailers. In their shrewdness, they are rebellious against authority.

"Wealth and honor come from you; you are the ruler of all things. In your hands are strength and power to exalt and give strength to all." (1 Chronicles 29:12; 12 NIV)

"By humility and the fear of the Lord Are riches and honor and life, "(Proverbs 22:4; NKJV)

"Length of days is in her right hand, in her left hand riches and honor."(Proverbs 3:16; NKJV)

CHAPTER 10

THE PRACTICE AND BLESSINGS OF HONOR

"Now when she came to the man of God at the hill, she caught him by the feet, but Gehazi came near to push her away. But the man of God said, "Let her alone; for her soul is in deep distress, and the Lord has hidden it from me, and has not told me." 37: So she went in, fell at his feet, and bowed to the ground; then she picked up her son and went out." [90]

"Honor is given to a man with and under authority."
Bishop Solomon Mukonjo

Honor is not a theological doctrine dancing about in our heads, but a life we should live with one another as children of the same household. However, we cannot just wake up one day and know how to honor one another. We grow through practice. In His house, God has stored up blessings that come with kingdom honor.

Biblical Perspective

Even though most of the scriptures we studied largely depict the physical acts of honor toward one another, it is not limited to these

---

[90] 2 Kings 4:27,37; New King James Version

alone as we shall see through this chapter. Furthermore, honor also goes as far as honoring oneself by the quality and life of discipline you live.

Honoring parents[91]

Exodus 20:12: "Honor your father and your mother, that your days may be long upon the land which the LORD your God is giving you." (NKJV)

The first time the word "honor" is mentioned in the bible, it is in regard to parents and has a promise of long life attached to it. The second blessing is; "So that it may be well with you". This means that honoring one's parents leads to success, prosperity, health and peace.

This particular commandment is reiterated by Moses, Jesus and Paul (representing the old covenant and the prophets and the new covenant and the apostles). In Matthew 15:4-6, Jesus said that whoever refuses to help their parents by giving excuses that what they have is an offering to God are not honoring them. Parents also ought to honor their children by not provoking them to wrath. They should instead bring them up in the ways of the Lord. This is the beauty of the new covenant; everyone is included. It is also a confirmation that honor is not a one-way traffic.

Honoring the household of faith

1 Timothy 5:1-2: "Do not rebuke an older man harshly, but exhort him as if he were your father. Treat younger men as brothers, 2 older women as mothers, and younger women as sisters, with absolute purity (NIV)."

When my mother was still alive, she taught my siblings and I never to call any older person by their name. We had to devise means of addressing older people without using their names. We called elders "uncle" or "auntie". The essence in this was to teach us to honor people. Older women were referred to as mums while the older men were "sirs". Our age mates were either "a brother" or "a sister". This is what Paul taught Timothy his spiritual son in the verse above. "With all purity" makes the instruction stricter and in this case, the Spirit of God encouraged the young man not to make any sexual advances to

---

[91] Deuteronomy 5:16; Matthew 15:4; Ephesian 6:1-2

sisters in the Lord or use his pastoral position to take advantage of the younger women in his congregation.

While growing up, God led some of my friends and I to sit under Apostle Alex Mitala's youth camps in Entebbe, Uganda. Through these camps, we learnt the value of sexual abstinence and purity. As we went along singing (we had a music band), we were strong advocates and activists for the same. We recorded an audio album promoting sexual abstinence among young people. Without disregarding the numerous sexual temptations, we faced as young men, we still treated the younger women as our sisters and honored each other (we were an all-male music group) as brothers. This happened until we each got married and had our own families. This should be the life of honor for every young person today.

Doubly honoring those who labor among us

1 Thessalonians 5:12-13: And we urge you, brethren, to recognize those who labor among you, and are over you in the Lord and admonish you, 13 and to esteem them very highly in love for their work's sake. Be at peace among yourselves, (NKJV)."

1 Corinthians 9:1-2: "Am I not an apostle? Am I not free? Have I not seen Jesus Christ our Lord? Are you not my work in the Lord? 2 If I am not an apostle to others, yet doubtless I am to you. For you are the seal of my apostleship in the Lord (NKJV)."

1 Timothy 5:17-18: "Let the elders who rule well be counted worthy of double honor, especially those who labor in the word and doctrine. 18 For the Scripture says, "You shall not muzzle an ox while it treads out the grain," and, "The laborer is worthy of his wages (NKJV).

2 Chronicles 20:20-21: So they rose early in the morning and went out into the Wilderness of Tekoa; and as they went out, Jehoshaphat stood and said, "Hear me, O Judah and you inhabitants of Jerusalem: Believe in the Lord your God, and you shall be established; believe His prophets, and you shall prosper (NKJV)."

129

Those who labor in the word among us are the apostles, prophets, evangelists, pastors and teachers. These men [and women] are to be counted worthy to receive double honor, but how much is double honor? Honor comes from a Greek word that means, "a value, i.e. money paid, or (concretely and collectively) valuables, by analogy, esteem (especially of the highest degree), or the dignity itself." Reward comes from a Greek word that means, "pay for services [literally or figuratively], good or bad)." With that background, I conclude that you cannot honor a person you cannot give to. The extent to which you value them will determine the price of your gifts. How much do you think a person worthy of double honor is worth? What they are worth in your eyes is what you will give them. Their value will be reflected in your gifts to them. It is as plain as that. Honor leads us into believing in the LORD our God and we are established. However, we must believe His prophets so that we prosper. There is a blessing of prosperity that is tied to kingdom honor. When we honor those the LORD has set before us, we partake of the same prosperity that is tied to their callings and gifting.

> **❝Christians tend to reject people with the prophetic gift. Even Jesus was rejected and the title He used while citing this rejection was "prophet"❞**

Receiving those Christ has sent

John 13:20: Most assuredly, I say to you, he who receives whoever I send receives Me; and he who receives Me receives Him who sent Me, (NKJV)."

Matt 10:40-41: "He who receives you receives Me, and he who receives Me receives Him who sent Me. He who receives a prophet in the name of a prophet shall receive a prophet's reward. And he who receives a righteous

130

man in the name of a righteous man shall receive a righteous man's reward (NKJV)."

When we receive those that Jesus has sent, according to their callings/gifting (apostle, prophet, evangelist, pastor and teacher – [this is the key here: you must have a revelation of what gift you are receiving from and how you approach it]), we receive Him through them. In so doing, we also receive the calling's exact "pay for services" that they also receive from the Lord.

And as we receive Jesus through those He sends, we receive the Father who sent Jesus! Isn't that shocking to some of us? But another person will argue that how will they receive someone they are not sure that they have actually been sent by Christ. To which I answer, "You must exercise discernment (that we have looked at earlier)". Christians tend to reject people with the prophetic gift. Even Jesus was rejected and the title He used while citing this rejection was "prophet". Are we part of those who "kill, crucify and scourge" prophets?

Honorable conduct

1 Peter 2:11-12: Beloved, I beg you as sojourners and pilgrims, abstain from fleshly lusts which war against the soul, 12 having your conduct honorable among the Gentiles, that when they speak against you as evildoers, they may, by your good works which they observe, glorify God in the day of visitation (NKJV)."

2 Corinthians 8:20-21:"Avoiding this: that anyone should blame us in this lavish gift which is administered by us - 21 providing honorable things, not only in the sight of the Lord, but also in the sight of men (NKJV)."

Living a life of honor before God and men gives glory to Him. It is through our good works which men observe that they glorify the God we profess. Inspired by the Holy Spirit, the Apostle Peter tells us to be honorable among the gentiles so that they do not speak against us as evildoers. The opposite of good works are the fleshly lusts which war against the soul. We must abstain from them.

131

Treating everyone like a royal

We have already learnt that believers are kings and priests in the kingdom of God. I shall conclude that because each of us is a king in their own right, we must treat each other like the royals we are. We should give like kings give. Apostle (for this is who he is by calling) Moses Mukisa who prefers to go by his nick-name; Mosze, the leader of Worship Harvest Ministries in Kampala, and one of my mentors has a great teaching called, "The Generosity of Kings". When I listened to him teach, it opened my eyes to royal treatment. I learnt to give like a king. I give quality and costly things because I honor the people I give to.

Another couple that knows how to treat people like royalty are Apostle Charlie and Pastor Vikki Ammons of Restoration Christian Church Virginia. In their house, apart from the excellent neatness, cleanliness and order, they have what they call the "Bishop's Chambers"; an apartment that was exclusively prepared to host men and women of God from around the globe.

This apartment is like a hotel room, fully furnished, with a jacuzzi, a huge screen, a heater, a king-sized bed, and a very good interior design. When you are there, you feel like a member of the royal family. This is in contrast to a certain couple that I heard about, who did abominable things to kingdom royals who visited them.

It is said that, in order to test the humility of a man of God from Africa, they intentionally put him to sleep in their dog's room. And that if he refused or complained, then they would know that he had failed the test and they would not work with him. To this couple I ask, why would you test someone's humility like that? Why not just discern them?

The relationship Africans have with animals is different from the relationship Westerners have with pets. Putting a man of God from Africa in a dog's room is humiliating and dishonoring him in unimaginable ways.

Commending and recognizing others

Romans 16:1-2: "I commend to you Phoebe our sister, who is a servant of the church in Cenchrea, 2 that you may receive her in the Lord in a manner worthy of the saints, and assist her in whatever business she has need of you; for indeed she has been a helper of many and of myself also. Romans 16:7; Greet Andronicus and Junia, my countrymen and my fellow prisoners, who are of note among the apostles, who also were in Christ before me, (NKJV)."

Whenever my spiritual father addressed our singing band during a meeting or when he needed to give us an instruction, he always called us by name. He never generalized anyone, but made each one of us feel special.

At 70 years, he still does not forget names, and even addresses people that he has met for the first time by their name. This is what commending and recognition is all about, and Paul was also very good at it.

Honoring God with our bodies

1 Corinthians 6:19-20: "Do you not know that your body is a temple of the Holy Spirit, who is in you, whom you have received from God? You are not your own; 20 you were bought at a price. Therefore, honor God with your body." (NIV)

1 Thessalonians 4:3-5: "For this is the will of God, your sanctification: that you should abstain from sexual immorality; 4 that each of you should know how to possess his own vessel in sanctification and honor, 5 not in passion of lust, like the Gentiles who do not know God." (NKJV)

God has honored us so much and made us His dwelling place. We should, therefore, honor Him by keeping our bodies free from sexual immorality. Our bodies are not ours anymore. Our bodies belong to Christ and we should be good stewards of them.

Learning to walk in self-control over our bodies and their desires in sanctification and honor is pleasing unto the Lord. It is His will toward us.

133

Pleasing one another

Romans 15:1-3: "We who are strong ought to bear with the failings of the weak and not to please ourselves. 2 Each of us should please his neighbor for his good, to build him up. 3 For even Christ did not please himself but, as it is written: "The insults of those who insult you have fallen on me." (NIV)

Even Christ did not please Himself, but suffered for us instead of saving Himself. Therefore, we ought to please others over our own interests, carrying the burdens of the weaker brethren. Pleasing others for their good builds them up, and in turn cures our selfishness.

Employer and employee relations

1 Timothy 6:1-2: Let as many bondservants as are under the yoke count their own masters worthy of all honor, so that the name of God and His doctrine may not be blasphemed. 2 And those who have believing masters, let them not despise them because they are brethren, but rather serve them because those who are benefited are believers and beloved. Teach and exhort these things (NKJV).

The name of the Lord can be put to shame if a believer is disobedient and rebellious to his employers. Late coming, failure to follow through with assignments and projects, under delivering, wasting a lot of time on social media and the like do not honor the name of the Lord. On the other hand, the Spirit of God admonishes believing employers to also treat their employees with honor. Not just boss them around using their positions and titles, but to lead them through humility and honor.

This should apply to the people that work in our homes. How do we treat our home affairs' managers (nannies)? How much do we pay them in relation to the load of work they do on top of looking after our children? What names do we call them? Where do they sit during meal time? On the dining with us or alone in the corridors and corners of the house? Do we share toilets with them or do we fear that they will infect us with diseases? How much do we pay the security personnel who also doubles as the landscaper, gardener and waste manager (garbage collection) in our homes? Do we invite them to eat with us or do they have cook their own "special" meal? Do we serve them enough of everything or do we deprive them by giving them little? Is there some special foods that we do not allow them to eat? Godliness should start in our own homes before we take it to our churches.

Civil responsibility

1 Timothy 2:1-2: "Therefore, I exhort first of all that supplications, prayers, intercessions, and giving of thanks be made for all men, 2 for kings and all who are in authority, that we may lead a quiet and peaceable life in all godliness and reverence." (NKJV)

1 Peter 2:17:" Honor all people. Love the brotherhood. Fear God. Honor the king (NKJV).

In 2011 when Uganda held general presidential elections, I got carried away by my desire to see a new president that I began advocating for change and campaigning for the politician I wanted to win. Sadly, I sometimes sounded radical on my Facebook wall. Two people that I honor corrected me through Facebook messenger that my role as a believer was to pray and to secretly vote for the person I thought would be good to lead my country instead of publicly criticizing the ruling government. As believers, we can speak against injustice, but in an honorable way. Dr. Martin Luther King Jnr is a great example of a believer who spoke and fought against injustice honorably without violence. The results of praying for our leaders, standing for elective political positions, and voting are peace and quietness reigning in the land. When this happens, the gospel will have free course to be preached

❝Many Christians do not even want to vote, but complain when bad leaders are elected into government❞

135

unhindered.

Unfortunately, many Christians do not even want to vote, but complain when bad leaders are elected into government. Fear God. Honor the King. Participate in politics. Cast your vote. Live a peaceful non-violent life. The government of Uganda recently came up with one of the weirdest ideas ever! They levied a tax on social media usage and passed it into a law. In addition to paying taxes on cell phones, talk and data credit, we also have to part with a tax to access Facebook, Twitter, WhatsApp and the like. A total of over 20 apps were to be taxed on use. Almost all social media users in Uganda installed Virtual Private Network (VPN) services and apps to access social media without paying the taxes. As an IT professional, I would have done the same, but because I am learning to honor the state, I chose to pay the ridiculous taxes!

Husbands and Wives

1 Peter 3:1,5-7: "In the same way, you wives, be submissive to your own husbands [subordinate, not as inferior, but out of respect for the responsibilities entrusted to husbands and their accountability to God, and so partnering with them] so that even if some do not obey the word [of God], they may be won over [to Christ] without discussion by the godly lives of their wives, 5 For in this way in former times the holy women, who hoped in God, used to adorn themselves, being submissive to their own husbands and adapting themselves to them; 6 just as Sarah obeyed Abraham [following him and having regard for him as head of their house], calling him lord. And you have become her daughters if you do what is right without being frightened by any fear [that is, being respectful toward your husband but not giving in to intimidation, nor allowing yourself to be led into sin, nor to be harmed]. 7 In the same way, you husbands, live with your wives in an understanding way [with great gentleness and tact, and with an intelligent regard for the marriage relationship], as with someone physically weaker, since she is a woman. Show her honor and respect as a fellow heir of the grace of life, so that your prayers will not be hindered or ineffective (AMP)."

With the prevalence of male chauvinism, independent women, emancipation campaigns, sexual liberation, alternative lifestyles, drag queens, the porn industry, Hollywood, and a move away from fundamental Christian beliefs to liberalism; the relationship between men and women has also changed over the years. The number of single, separated or divorced parents are also rising every day. The biblical family structure is being redefined by liberal laws, lifestyles and culture. Scriptures have a solution to the above problems if we take heed.

Wives are admonished to be submissive and subordinate, adapting themselves to their own husbands. Women should not act as inferiors, but should submit out of respect for the responsibility entrusted to them. Sarah obeyed Abraham, calling him "Lord", not out of fear, but out of high regard as head of their house. "Lord" comes from a Hebrew word, transliterated as "adown", and is a masculine noun. It literally means; *"firm, strong, lord, master, superintendent of household affairs, king, husband, prophet, governor, prince, father, priest, theophany angel, captain, and general recognition of superiority."* [92]

How many women look at their husbands like that? How many relate to them like they would to such individuals? Husbands are instructed to live with their wives with wisdom and understanding. However, this understanding has to have profound gentleness and tact. A husband should have an intelligent regard for his marriage, knowing that his marriage to his wife is "unto the Lord". Men are admonished to honor and respect their wives as fellow heirs of the grace of eternal life. According to this scripture, women are not slaves, inferior, or sex objects. They are not property to be owned. However, they are fellow partners, heirs, kings, priests, apostles, prophets, evangelists, pastors and teachers in Christ. Haven't you seen women whose marriages fail, but they go ahead to succeed in all other fields including ministry? It is partly because they are as gifted as men in other areas and can flourish the same way men do if the environment is conducive.

How many husbands treat their wives with the attitude this scripture supposes we should have for our wives? The last clause of this verse is scary. It warns men against the possibility of their prayers being

---

[92] Blue Letter Bible. Lexixon Results. Strong's H113 – 'adown. Retrieved from down http://www. blbclassic.org/lang/lexicon/lexicon.cfm?Strongs=H113&cscs=Zec on 16/10/2018 at 07:16am

hindered or becoming ineffective if they mistreat their wives in any way.

It does not matter how prayerful a man is, or how committed in the ministry they are. If they do not treat their wives as Christ treats His bride, their prayers, commitment to ministry and devotion will be hindered and ineffective. They will yield no results. Wow! The wife should not wait for her husband to love them so that they submit a hundred percent, neither should the husband wait for the wife to submit so that he loves her a hundred percent. Whatever each of them does should be done in honor to the Lord. None of them should set terms and conditions before fulfilling their God-given obligations and responsibilities of their marriages.

Agreeing to disagree and resolving conflict honorably

In the book of Acts 18:24-28, there is a story of a man called Apollos who was instructed in the way of the Lord. He was bold, eloquent in speech, mighty in scriptures, fervent in spirit and accurate in the ways of the Lord. The only problem was that he only knew the baptism of John. When Aquilla and Priscilla heard him, they honored him by taking him aside privately and expounded the way of God more accurately to him. When you have an issue with someone, instead of posting those feelings and emotions on social media, it is more honorable to agree to disagree. Lovingly confront and resolve any conflict and honor one another instead of making hypocritical posts and statuses on social media. If you fear confrontation, please refrain from any insinuative posts and comments on social media about people or situations.

Honoring the LORD with our substance
Proverbs 3:9-10; Honor the LORD with your possessions, And with the firstfruits of all your increase; 10 So your barns will be filled with plenty, And your vats will overflow with new wine." (NKJV)

Where someone's treasure is, there their heart will be. If we cannot honor the LORD with our possessions and the first fruits of ALL our increase, there is no way we are going to experience an overflow of blessings and prosperity. I started to consistently honor the LORD with a first fruit offering (the very first income I would get in a new year) in 2015, the overflow of different blessings has been tremendous in my life, family and ministry.

Refraining from ministerial advantages and benefits

2 Thessalonians 3:7-10: "For you yourselves know how you ought to follow our example. We were not idle when we were with you, 8 nor did we eat anyone's food without paying for it. On the contrary, we worked night and day, laboring and toiling so that we would not be a burden to any of you. 9 We did this, not because we do not have the right to such help, but in order to make ourselves a model for you to follow. 10 For even when we were with you, we gave you this rule: "If a man will not work, he shall not eat." (NIV)

1 Thessalonians 2:9-10 "Surely you remember, brothers, our toil and hardship; we worked night and day in order not to be a burden to anyone while we preached the gospel of God to you. 10 You are witnesses, and so is God, of how holy, righteous and blameless we were among you who believed." (NKJV)

This is the highest form of honor a man of God can give to the flock; refraining from receiving what they should have been entitled to. This is what Paul did with the assembly at Thessalonica. The reasons he did this are as follows:

- He did not want to be a burden to anyone while preaching the gospel.
- He wanted to be an example and model for hard work among the believers.
- To teach believers that paying for your own food is more honorable than getting free things.
- That there were repercussions for laziness and idleness.

Sometimes it is more honorable for a minister of God to refuse certain ministerial privileges for the sake of the gospel if he senses that he might be enslaved by the benefits or he might become a burden to the people. There is nothing dishonoring to a man of God as depending on people for his sustenance. No wonder Paul made tents. Two men of God come to mind on this point; Pastor Rick Warren of Saddleback

Church in USA and Pastor Joseph Prince of New Creation Church in Singapore. Out of their free will, Pastor Rick refunded ALL the money he had ever received as salary for the previous years (over 25) to his church, and Pastor Joseph Prince also asked to be removed from his church's payroll a few years ago.

Should spiritual entities also be honored?

Jude 8-9: "Likewise also these dreamers defile the flesh, reject authority, and speak evil of dignitaries. 9 Yet Michael the archangel, in contending with the devil, when he disputed about the body of Moses, dared not bring against him a reviling accusation, but said,"The Lord rebuke you! (NKJV)."

Revelation 19:10: "At this I fell at his feet to worship him. But he said to me, "Do not do it! I am a fellow servant with you and with your brothers who hold to the testimony of Jesus. Worship God! For the testimony of Jesus is the spirit of prophecy (NIV)."

Jude verses 8-9 is a remarkable scripture that speaks about evil men that reject authorities and speak evil of dignitaries. The Holy Spirit through Jude mentions the devil as an example of a dignitary! What is the essence of this scripture? It is to teach us not to be careless with our words even when we are confronting the devil through spiritual warfare. There has been a tendency in some charismatic and Pentecostal circles for the so-called "prayer warriors", especially in developing countries, to insult the devil with all kinds of vulgar words. My friend's grandmother comes to mind. This old mama has the liberty of using abusive and vulgar words towards the devil during her prayer escapades.

If the archangel Michael did not use abusive language in contending with the devil concerning Moses' body, how dare we insult him? We do not contend with the devil on our own, but in the Lord's name. When we use reviling accusations and insults against the devil, he mocks and laughs at our ignorance! On the flip side of it, in Revelation 19:10, John the beloved tried to prostrate and worship before an angel, but the angel restrained him because he was his fellow servant. Even though we should not insult the devil, we must not at the same time prostrate before or worship God's angels that he sends to us. Only God is to be worshiped, not other beings (whether physical or spiritual).

Why some people may not practice Honor

Throughout scriptures, there are instances when people refused to honor those God had sent. There are a number of reasons why certain people will just refuse to give honor where it is due. In so doing, they will unconsciously hinder the blessings that come with it. Let's look at some of them, using scriptures.

Matthew 13:57-58: "When He had come to His own country, He taught them in their synagogue, so that they were astonished and said, "Where did this Man get this wisdom and these mighty works? 55 Is this not the carpenter's son? Is not His mother called Mary? And His brothers James, Joses, Simon, and Judas? 56 And His sisters, are they not all with us? Where then did this Man get all these things?" 57 So they were offended at Him. But Jesus said to them, "A prophet is not without honor except in his own country and in his own house." 58 Now He did not do many mighty works there because of their unbelief." (NKJV)

Mark 6:4-6: "But Jesus said to them, "A prophet is not without honor except in his own country, among his own relatives, and in his own house." 5 Now He could do no mighty work there, except that He laid His hands on a few sick people and healed them. 6 And He marveled because of their unbelief. Then He went about the villages in a circuit, teaching." (NKJV)

John 4:44-45: "For Jesus Himself testified that a prophet has no honor in his own country." (NKJV)

Indifference: When people are generally heartless, cold-hearted, aloof, withdrawn and detached towards certain gifts, especially apostles and prophets they are not being honorable. Indifference rejects spiritual reality set right before our very eyes.

Familiarity: This happens when people become indifferent by virtue of being familiar with their leaders or fellow brethren. This blinds their eyes to recognizing the gift and calling of God upon an individual for reasons such as; growing up with them, being friends, age-mates, tribe-mates, acquaintances, sharing a history together, among others. "Familiarity breeds contempt", goes the proverb.

Contempt: The feeling that a particular minister/gift is worthless or beneath consideration. This also takes in those that think that certain gifts ceased to operate with the early church, so anyone who claims to be an apostle or prophet, for instance, is held in contempt.

Ridicule: Language or behavior intended to mock or humiliate those that God has set before us in the gospel, especially those gifted differently than us.

Scorn: Open disrespect for and looking down on those that God has called in the ministry. Some educated and highly-placed people, especially in third world countries think that ministers of God first failed in life then resorted to "easy things of" preaching the gospel. Such people will not regard servants of God with honor.

Offence: Emotional hurt, being upset, annoyance caused by misunderstanding, misjudging or misapplying a ministers' actions, words or conduct.

Ignorance about a particular gift, subject, or minister will also hinder people from walking in honor towards others and those God has set before them.

Unbelief: A rejection of belief and faith either towards what men of God teach, what they do, or entirely towards God. All of us have places of unbelief; it is the levels that differ. With any of the above mental attitudes and strongholds, we can never receive any ministry from those that we hold them against.

Getting Practical with Kingdom Honor
The following is not a "to-do" list, but just suggestions that can help us as we cultivate, build, and maintain a culture of honor in the kingdom.

- Be willing to be discipled, mentored or fathered in the Lord (Philippians 2:19-20, 21).
- Be accountable to three kinds of people in your life:

1) – A "Paul"; a father figure working as a discipler, mentor or spiritual father in your life. Their age does not matter.

2) A "Barnabas"; a fellow soldier in the gospel. An accountability partner, a friend who sticks closer than a brother.

3) A "Timothy"; a son in the Lord, your disciple and your mentee.

- Sympathize, empathize and have compassion on others (Philippians 4:26).
- Choose to lead by example. Take the first initiative in all things. Be the first to give, the first to love, the first to make the call, to send that email, to send the text. Show the way.
- Leave the toilet cleaner than you found it. Honor its next user.
- Keep your house clean, neat and tidy. Honor your family members and your visitors through a clean environment. Our houses and homes should reflect who we truly are in the spirit; pure and holy. Cluttered, messed up and disorganized houses reflect the state of our souls.
- Shave (mostly men), take a bath/shower. Honor your body as God's temple. Don't depend on perfumes and deodorant to replace bathing. Swimming is not bathing. Mints cannot replace brushing of teeth.
- Keep time and be on time. Honor appointments, follow through with schedules, events and calendars. Finish projects and work plans. RSVP has a purpose, let's use it, at least a week before the event.
- Serve, serve, serve, serve others first.
- Help the vulnerable people you meet in malls, at airports, in restaurants or any other public places. Carry their luggage, push their cart, open doors for them and anything you can find to do.
- When you visit friends or family, carry something with you. If you are to spend a night, wake up early and help clean or do dishes.

- When you host someone, let them acknowledge that you put in effort in preparing. Clean up and unclutter the room to give it some breathing space. Please scrub the bathroom and toilet. Unless otherwise, pick them up or drop them off yourself (more honorable if you do this with your spouse). Make them a comfortable and clean bed, its size does not matter.
- When you receive any post, comment or email that puts someone in a negative light, please do not re-share it. Delete it. Don't just share everything you receive or see on social media. Some of those posts are "stage-managed" to create a buzz (good or bad). You will not be fined if you don't comment on every post.
- Say 'Yes' or 'No'. Stand by one of those words and keep it. Integrity has no "maybes", "I will try" or "I will see".
- After you have helped someone, shut up.
- Keep what the Lord shows you in other people's lives private. Be a good steward of God's secrets, He will trust you with more.
- When you make a mistake, apologize properly. Saying "okay" I am sorry means that you are not. Own up, swallow your pride and speak in the first person: "I am sorry, please forgive me", and mean it. If it's fake, we shall still know by the Spirit.
- Tip. Tip. Tip Big. Leave the change with the waitress, the taxi operator, the boda boda (a motorcycle used as a mode of transport in some African countries).
- Worn out, torn, beaten down, dirty and smelly clothes should not be donated. Honor and value people, their lack does not mean that they are worthless. The same applies to other items put up for donation. Give quality gifts.
- For the missionaries that go to third world countries, candy, chocolates and sweets are not needs for poor children. What they really need is education, medical care, clean water, small decent houses and good clothes and shoes.
- Be polite and courteous. Say, "Please", "Thank you", and "Excuse me" Unless someone tells you that they are okay

144

with going by their first names, sir and ma'am should be the norm.
- Confrontation, if healthy, is more beneficial than hypocrisy and gossip.
- Draw out the beauty and importance of each person through affirmation, commendation and public approval.
- Honor friendships. Keep away from backbiting, gossip, maliciousness, and blackmail.
- Even in a disagreement, keep your voice down. Man's anger does not produce God's righteousness.
- Treat children, the disabled, the elderly and expectant mothers with tenderness.
- Stand up when a distinguished person walks into the room or reaches out his or her hand to greet you. After their appearance, give them a standing ovation.
- This is for motorists in developing countries: zebra crossings mean that drivers stop for passengers to cross roads. Don't just drive without honoring pedestrians. Allow them to cross.

How should it be done? How do we Celebrate those God has set before us? How about those religious groups that venerate men of God and the saints? Are there extreme acts of honor that should be rejected? Let us delve into our final discussion and find out.

"Honor is a deep, deep abiding inner attitude of reverence and respect." [93]

----

[93] From the Sermon: "To Whom Honor is Due: The Fifth Commandment" By Martin G. Collins given on 14/07/2001. Retrieved from https://www.cgg.org/index.cfm/fuseaction/Audio.details/ID/656/To-Whom-Honor-Is-Due.htm on 16/10/2018 at 6:28pm

CHAPTER 11

CELEBRATION, VENERATION AND EXTREMES

"When the men were returning home after David had killed the Philistine, the women came out from all the towns of Israel to meet King Saul with singing and dancing, with joyful songs and with timbrels and lyres. 7 As they danced, they sang: "Saul has slain his thousands, and David his tens of thousands." [94]

"A very large crowd spread their cloaks on the road, while others cut branches from the trees and spread them on the road. 9 The crowds that went ahead of him and those that followed shouted, "Hosanna to the Son of David!" "Blessed is he who comes in the name of the Lord!" "Hosanna in the highest heaven!" [95]

Celebration: Acceptable Honor

It is an unconscious belief in Christian culture that if we celebrate the people God has set before us, they will swell with pride. Out of fear, we try as much as possible not to give or receive any kind of celebration because we want to "be humble". It is indeed true that there are people who take celebration to the opposite direction.

However, a minister of God, with or without celebration, must be fully secure in themselves. They should know their place and position in the Lord, that whether they are celebrated or not, nothing changes

[94] 1 Samuel 18:6-7, New International Version
[95] Matthew 21:1-11, New International Version

in their disposition and outlook. That said, I want to submit scriptural evidence of instances where people celebrated the servants of God because of what the LORD had done through them. In 1 Samuel chapter 18, after David had killed Goliath and secured a victory for Israel over the Philistines in the previous chapter, something interesting happed. As the fighters entered Israel, the women came out of the towns to meet King Saul. They had composed celebration songs and as they danced, they said: "Saul has slain his thousands and David his tens of thousands". This did not go down well with Saul because in his mind it elevated David above him. The chapter does not show whether David was with King Saul at that time, or whether he received or rejected this celebration. However, verses 18 and 22 reveal David's humble heart. He did not consider himself merited to become the king's son-in-Law.

This portion of scripture teaches us that whether we are celebrated or not, we should always keep an attitude of humility in our hearts (because that is where God searches). On the other hand, a person might reject celebration, yet they are prideful in their hearts. They might crave to be celebrated like Saul did and feel envious if someone else is celebrated more than they are. There's nothing sinful in giving or receiving celebration. Matthew 21:1-11 gives us a story about Jesus entering Jerusalem. Although this was in fulfilment of prophecy, I have already asserted that very few people (mostly his inner circle of disciples) knew who Jesus really was. In dealing with Jesus, the multitudes, for the most part, felt they were dealing with a prophet or a man.

Therefore, as he approached Jerusalem on a colt, the crowds spread their cloaks while others cut down tree branches for him to walk on. Jesus received the celebration because He knew its spiritual significance. He knew that he was coming in the name of the LORD, therefore he did not feel that he was "taking the LORD's glory". His heart was right, so he did not need to reject the celebration.

In Luke 19:39-40, the Pharisees thought that the celebration was unwarranted and extreme. They did not receive Jesus as He who had come in the name of the LORD. They asked Him to rebuke

148

His disciples. However, Jesus did not rebuke them. He received the celebration wholesomely because it held a spiritual significance. I propose that as long as the person being celebrated has their heart right with God and has no guile, bitterness, or pride, they can receive any kind of celebration if it has a spiritual significance (and only they can tell whether it does or not). If the world celebrates its own, why shouldn't the body of Christ celebrate her own?

How about Security and Protocol details for "men of God"?

This is another very sensitive area. Let me first state that for as long as the security detail and protocol is not for pomp or making the minister of God inaccessible, it is my personal opinion that there is a growing need to create some order and take security precautions even in the Body of Christ.

On Saturday October 27, 2018, a white supremacist attacked and shot at Jews in a Synagogue in Pittsburg, Pennsylvania, killing at least 11 of them and injuring about seven more during a Sabbath celebration service. He was unapologetic and unremorseful.[96]

In 2017, a pastor of Ugandan origin living and serving in South Africa had just finished preaching when he entered his office to quickly prepare for the next service. About three people requested to see him "briefly" before he went in for the second service and as soon as they entered his office, they immediately shot him. He died as his church's ministers took him to hospital.[97]

In September 2018, a young "upcoming" pastor of Church of God in Prophecy in Jamaica was shot dead in the middle of his sermon by a lone gunman.[98]

In February 2016, in Dayton Ohio, a pastor of St. Peter's Missionary Baptist Church was allegedly killed by his own brother, in the middle of

---

[96] The New York Times. 27/10/2018. 11 Killed in Synagogue Massacre; Suspect charged with 29 Counts. Retrrieved from https://www.nytimes.com/2018/10/27/us/active-shooter-pittsburgh-synagogue-shooting.html on 01/11/2018 at 6:45am.

[97] I heard this story from his very brother early in the year of the publication of this book.

[98] The Star. Pastor shot dead in church by Alicia Barrett (September 21, 2018). Retrieved from http://jamaica-star.com/article/news/20180921/pastor-shot-dead-church on 16/10/2018 at 08:15pm

the service while he sat at the pulpit with his choir.[99]

In 2015 in Charleston, a 21-year-old white supremacist murdered nine African Americans during a prayer service at Emanuel African Methodist Episcopal Church in South Carolina.[100]

A mass shooting occurred at First Baptist Church in Sutherland Springs, Texas, where 26 people died and 20 were injured in November 2017.[101]
We can go on and on about the various religious-related shootings that have occurred over the years.

From Islamic Fundamentalists like Boko Haram attacking churches and killing believers in Nigeria,[102] to other shootings in the USA.[103] The need for some kind of security in Christian congregations is growing. In the USA, almost all churches have a security system for their buildings. In the South where I have visited, and had an opportunity to minister, some churches have security teams whose armed members sit scattered across the entire sanctuary, just in case an attack happens. Some pastors preach with "little" guns in their trousers. It is not that they live in fear; it is knowledge that the devil is real, and his biggest enemy is the Bride of Christ. Evil is in the world. *"We know that we are children of God, and that the whole world is under the control of the evil one,"* writes John in 1 John 5:19.

It does not matter whether those killed during Christian gatherings had personal issues they hadn't settled with their killers or not, the security and safety of congregants and men of God matters to God. I don't think He smiles when His children die in such ways. Most believers and ministers in developing countries see no need for a security and

[99] AJC. Police: Pastor Shot, Killed at Church. Retrieved from https://www.ajc.com/news/national/police-pastor-shot-killed-church/XtBnjd8cgieJMw520jj3zN/ on 16/10/2018 at 08:25pm
[100] Wikipedia. Charleston church shooting. 04/10/2018. Retrieved from https://en.wikipedia.org/wiki/Charleston_church_shooting on 16/10/2018 at 08:42pm
[101] Wikipedia. Sutherland Springs church shooting. 15/10/2018. Retrieved from https://en.wikipedia.org/wiki/Sutherland_Springs_church_shooting on 16/10/2018 at 08:55pm
[102] Wikipedia. List of Massacres in Nigeria. https://en.wikipedia.org/wiki/List_of_massacres_in_Nigeria
[103] The Salt Lake Tribune: https://www.sltrib.com/news/nation-world/2017/11/06/a-list-of-some-us-house-of-worship-shootings-since-2012/

protocol team as part of their ministry, arguing that it is God who protects them. This is true, but His protection can also be through people. Even when the LORD is Israeli's protection and security, giving them victory over their enemies, the nation has always had an army.

When God uses certain vessels tremendously, the devil also releases a host of spiritual and physical attacks against them. I think that security and protocol details can prevent some of the attacks against the servants of God. Security is a need, not a luxury or privilege. Protocol is mostly to maintain order and to prevent the ministers of the gospel from getting physically hurt if the crowds press in around them. When Jesus was thronged by multitudes (Mark 5:24, Luke 5:1), His disciples acknowledged and tried to control it. God's ministers are human and they can be suffocated by multitudes (especially prophetic, evangelistic, or apostolic individuals who walk in miracles, signs and wonders).

I cannot fail to mention that I acknowledge that prideful souls have misused this need thereby making it hard for people to access them. Their security details deny anyone an opportunity to be close to "men of God." Others regard themselves as demi-gods, surrounded by security details that literally make them inaccessible. Some have a security detail that is almost as that of a country's president. Anything can be misused; this, I agree.

Veneration and Extrimism: when honor should be rejected

There are scenarios when honor should be rejected. This is the kind of honor that pumps someone up and makes them feel like demi-gods. Scriptures are also not silent on these and as we come to the close of this discussion, we shall look at scenarios when honor should be rejected.

John 5:41-44: "I do not receive honor from men. 42 But I know you, that you do not have the love of God in you. 43 I have come in My Father's name, and you do not receive Me; if another comes in his own name, him you will receive."

151

If one feels that the honor being given to them is extreme, they should reject it. They are not obligated to receive it if they do not feel comfortable with it. In John chapter 5, Jesus rejected honor from those that did not believe in Him. Those that do not have the love of God in them cannot honor those that God has sent. It is impossible. We, too, ought to reject that kind of honor.

> *John 6:15: "Therefore when Jesus perceived that they were about to come and take Him by force to make Him king, He departed again to the mountain by Himself alone."*

In John chapter 6, Jesus refused to be made king by force. He knew that He hadn't come to become an earthly King. He rejected that honor, yet in the triumphant entry, he accepted to be treated as a King! Those who try to take men and women of God into gifts and callings that are not theirs, and those who give undue and insincere honor should be rejected, too.

> *Luke 11:27-28: "And it happened, as He spoke these things, that a certain woman from the crowd raised her voice and said to Him, "Blessed is the womb that bore You, and the breasts which nursed You!" 28 But He said, "More than that, blessed are those who hear the word of God and keep it!"*

All through scripture and in the ministry, there are immature and spiritually ignorant people who idolize the gift of God upon ministers. They use careless words in the name of honoring them. These should be rebuked and corrected in love. They should be taught about the greater good of the ministry.

This is how Jesus responded to the woman who was trying to fix her focus on Mary His mother. He did not reject His mother's role, but rather showed the woman that there was a "more than that..." (Luke 11:27-28). There is always something more than mere honor to the vessel.

The fulfillment of God's divine purpose in their lives is more important than the gift upon them.

Acts 14:8-18: "And in Lystra a certain man without strength in his feet was sitting, a cripple from his mother's womb, who had never walked. 9 This man heard Paul speaking. Paul, observing him intently and seeing that he had faith to be healed, 10 said with a loud voice, "Stand up straight on your feet!" And he leaped and walked. 11 Now when the people saw what Paul had done, they raised their voices, saying in the Lycaonian language, "The gods have come down to us in the likeness of men!" 12 And Barnabas they called Zeus, and Paul, Hermes, because he was the chief speaker. 13 Then the priest of Zeus, whose temple was in front of their city, brought oxen and garlands to the gates, intending to sacrifice with the multitudes. But when the apostles Barnabas and Paul heard this, they tore their clothes and ran in among the multitude, crying out 15 and saying, "Men, why are you doing these things? We also are men with the same nature as you, and preach to you that you should turn from these useless things to the living God, who made the heaven, the earth, the sea, and all things that are in them, 16 who in bygone generations allowed all nations to walk in their own ways. 17 Nevertheless He did not leave Himself without witness, in that He did good, gave us rain from heaven and fruitful seasons, filling our hearts with food and gladness." 18 And with these sayings they could scarcely restrain the multitudes from sacrificing to them (NKJV)."

It is important to note that it is God's servant that should perceive that honor has become extreme, and thereby reject it. It is Jesus who perceived that they wanted to make him king by force and so he rejected it. It is Barnabas and Paul who heard that the people wanted to sacrifice to them that they stopped them, and not the other way around. On the other hand, what the spectator can term as extreme and idolatry might be an act of honor in the eyes of God, and the servant themselves. The story of Mary and the costly fragrant oil that she poured on the feet of Jesus proves this contention. Simon the host saw her as a waste and extreme extravagance while Jesus saw it as an act of honor which he received wholeheartedly.

In the story of Paul and Barnabas in Acts 14, even with their words, "they could scarcely restrain the multitudes from sacrificing to them." Sometimes it not easy to stop people from honoring God's servants in strange ways. However, these servants should try as much as possible, like Paul and Barnabas did, to restrain the people from doing certain things if they have perceived that that kind of honor is uncalled for. If God's servants perceive that their congregations want to venerate them as demi-gods, they want to pray or testify in their names instead of the name of Christ and prostrate before their statutes or pictures, they should reject it. This will save them, the ministry and the people from idolatry. No one should ever take the place of God.

It is wrong and dangerous to accept and receive undue and extreme honor because the anointing and the gifts, even if they are irrevocable, do not spring from you, but from the Spirit of God. They are given to you to serve others, not your own self. Rejecting of honor also depends on "how much" honor the man or woman of God is willing to receive. To some, even a mere mention of their names sends a river of pride in their souls. If God's servant cannot handle certain gestures of honor, they should reject them. However, that does not mean that another man of God cannot handle the kind of honor that the other rejected.

The place of Correction and Rebuke

If you do not have a relationship with someone, or if you are not an outstanding, blameless, credible leader in the Body of Christ, do not even think of starting to correct or rebuke those in error. It does not work that way. It will backfire, especially on you. Because the person you may want to rebuke or correct will become defensive and explosive. Even if we ought to honor one another, there is behavior (either with those being honored or those who do the "honoring") that must be corrected and rebuked by the household of faith. Jesus sets a precedent on the procedure of correction and rebuke.

> *Matthew 18:15-17 "Moreover if your brother sins against you, go and tell him his fault between you and him alone. If he hears you, you have gained your brother. 16 But if he will not hear, take with you one or two more, that 'by the mouth of two or three witnesses every word may be established.' 17 And if he refuses to hear them, tell it to the church. But if he refuses even to hear the church, let him be to you like a heathen and a tax collector." (NKJV)*

How many of us have followed Jesus' precedence revealed in the above scripture? Very few, I must say. What most of us do when a brother offends or sins is to criticize, slander and speak evil of them. We gossip about them, ridicule and blackmail them saying all kinds of things without verifying the facts or hearing their side of the story.

The precedent Jesus sets is that we must first go to that person and have a private and honorable conversation with them. If they hear you, you have saved them from their error. If they don't listen, Jesus says, then go with two or three other credible and honorable brethren and initiate another conversation. If, because of pride and deception they refuse to hear you, then call the bigger assembly of believers and share the issue. If the believer still refuses to listen to the body of believers, Jesus says let that person be like a non-believer. Basically, throw them out of your congregation! Excommunication is the word for it.

Paul reiterates the same thought in Titus 3:10-11; he says: *"Reject a divisive man after the first and second admonition, 11 knowing that such a person is warped and sinning, being self-condemned (NKJV)."* It is common that we first reject people before we even admonish them for the first time. The precedent Paul sets is that we can only reject a heretic after the first and second admonition (which means; calling to attention, mild rebuke or warning). Before we have admonished anyone, where do we get the boldness to go on social media and rant about them? Or make sermons out of them? When we do that, our error is actually bigger than theirs because we have not followed what the scripture teaches.

Paul says the same thing in Galatians 6:1 and 2 Thessalonians 3:13-15 respectively. He writes by the Spirit:
"Brethren, if a man is overtaken in any trespass, you who are spiritual restore such a one in a spirit of gentleness, considering yourself lest you also be tempted. 2 Bear one another's burdens, and so fulfill the law of Christ (NKJV)"....and "But as for you, brethren, do not grow weary in doing good. 14 And if anyone does not obey our word in this epistle, note that person and do not keep company with him, that he may be ashamed. 15 Yet do not count him as an enemy, but admonish him as a brother." (NKJV)

The person who ought to restore the one that has erred must be "more" spiritual than the one they are restoring. However, the spiritual person should restore through gentleness and carefulness lest they are also overtaken in the same fault. Carrying and bearing one another's burden is what restoration is actually all about. In the next scripture, Paul says that we should never get weary in well doing, and that if anyone walks in disobedience towards sound doctrine, they ought to be noted and separated against. Through this, they may be ashamed of their folly and turn around. However, we should not treat them as enemies, but as brothers that need to be admonished.

The Spirit, through Paul the apostle, says something similar in 1 Thessalonians 5:14-15: *"Now we exhort you, brethren, warn those who are unruly, comfort the fainthearted, uphold the weak, be patient with all. 15 See that no one renders evil for evil to anyone, but always pursue what is good both for yourselves and for all (NKJV)."*

He says, in essence, that the main motivation behind correction, rebuke, warning and admonition should be that we do not render evil for evil, but pursue what is good in everyone. If our motive is not to comfort the faint, uphold the weak and be patient with all, then we shouldn't be correcting anyone. The average Christian largely does the opposite. We discourage the faint and throw down the weak, we are impatient with anyone who does not grow at our pace. We pay evil for the evil weak people do to us. We don't pursue good in people, but only focus on their weaknesses, sins, and failures. In fact, if we think we are better than others and that we have the right to act that way towards them, we are being self-righteous.

James 5:19-20 says: *"Brethren, if anyone among you wanders from the truth, and someone turns him back, 20 let him know that he who turns a sinner from the error of his way will save a soul from death and cover a multitude of sins (NKJV)."*

Any motivation to expose other people's sins and failures springs from a pharisaic and self-righteous mentality. That aside, if done with humility, if we successfully turn anyone who has wandered from the truth back to the right tract we can save their souls from death. There is no need for a press release or mention of what transpired from our private meeting with those that went astray. Fruit is visible; if it's there, it will show.

Appendix I

Extra Reading List

1. Every Square Inch: An Introduction to Cultural Engagement for Christians. Lexham Press. Bruce Riley Ashford,

2. Spiritual Leadership: A Commitment to Excellence for Every Believer, Moody Publishers, 2007. J. Oswald Sanders

3. Culture of Honor: Sustaining a Supernatural Environment. Destiny Image Publishers, 2009. Danny Silk

4. The Church Life Model: A Biblical Pattern For The Spirit-Filled Church. Creation House. 2011. Illustrated Edition. Wayne and Sherry Lee

5. Church Shift: Revolutionize Your Life Faith, Church, and Life for the 21st Century. 2008. Charisma House. Sunday Adelaja